D0283768

Reaching for the World

Revealing Jesus as The Messiah in The Koran

By
Jeremiah Cummings
Evangelist & Author

Dedicated to
Bishop William C. Abney
Grand Rapids, Michigan

One Big Family Publishing

Contact info
Evangelist Jeremiah Cummings
P.O. Box 677276
Orlando, Florida. 32867

Phone: 866.294.WICC (9422)
E-mail: wicctv63@aol.com
Website: wicctv.org
ISBN 0-9770006-0-5

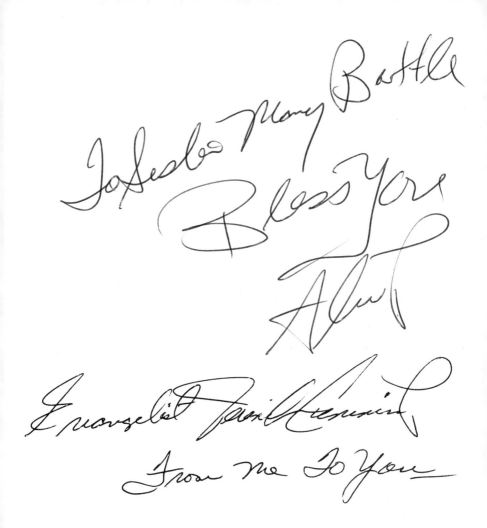

TABLE OF CONTENTS

Note: All scripture references King James Version
unless otherwise noted.

Book cover design by Web Vision Graphics,
www.webvisiongraphics.com.

INTRODUCTION

This book, *Reaching for the World*, I believe was a gift from God to me. It could only be by the Divine Spirit of an Awesome God that I could read, interpret, and compare the Muslim Koran with the Holy Bible, equip Christians, and be used to bring Muslims into the Kingdom of God. This book is designed to equip believers in Christ, with an understanding and knowledge that we've lacked for more than two thousand years, concerning the seed of Ishmael. Why would such a man like prophet Muhammad, of nearly fifteen hundred years ago, be raised up among the seed of Ishmael? And from the seed of Ishmael he came.

I pray that the world will see the open relationship of the seed of Ishmael and the children of Isaac, and it would understand that both of these nations fell headlong into the sin of idolatry. Remember also, that their father Abraham was called out from among his kindred, who were also heavily laden with idolatry. Muhammad came to his people after gaining knowledge of the Torah (first five books of Moses), and the Injil (the Gospel of Christ), to warn them of their idol worship, and to declare in their Arabic language that God is one (Deuteronomy 6:4).

The only problem occurred after Muhammad's death. The scholars of religion made the reformation of The Seed of Ishmael a religion and openly denied the virgin birth of Christ, his crucifixion, and his resurrection. I have been appointed in these last days to openly show the meaning of the Koran and the purpose of both Muhammad and THE CHRIST, so that men, women, and their children can return to the original plan of God from the beginning, and that is God's image and likeness in human form in this earth as it is in Heaven.

May you be blessed,
Evangelist Jeremiah Cummings

FOREWORD

The need to know what one believes in order to effectively defend the faith is of utmost importance. The message cannot merely be as the result of study and the borrowed knowledge of those with experience. But first-hand experience will indelibly brand the soul with a kind of knowledge enabling the witness to speak with deep conviction. God will guide one's life into avenues of experience, while the one experiencing such things is totally unaware of greater purpose. As the individual grows in understanding, he then is able to put into proper perspective events and challenges faced in life.

So it is with Evangelist Jeremiah Cummings who enjoyed a celebrated life in the field of entertainment, later to be personally mentored by Minister Louis Farrakhan and equipped to articulate both the Holy Bible and the Koran. God's mission for his life from the beginning was to make him into a vessel that would have the heart and qualifications in Reaching for the World with the timeless message of Jesus Christ whose transcendent character is irrefutably found in both the Bible and the Koran. He makes it clear that only through fully

3

accepting Jesus Christ as the only Savior and Messiah can one be truly saved.

I believe that this book will impact the lives of all who read it in a way as to compassionately minister to our brothers and sisters of the Muslim faith. It will help Christian believers to understand God's will for those who are honestly searching for the truth but might have settled a degree short of it. I trust that you will allow the message of Evangelist Cummings' life to help you articulate the message of the gospel to a religious but lost world. He is my friend, my brother and son in the Lord. I trust that his writings will present to you a perspective that would diffuse the tensions of strife without compromise between these two religions as Christ shines as, not only the example of holy living, but the life itself.

Woodrow Walker
Abundant Life Church

A Word from the Bishop

What an awesome word from God through such an anointed vessel. I am always looking for new ways to win souls to Christ. When I read Jeremiah Cummings book on reaching the world, I was excited to the point that I stayed up till 2:30 am reading this book. Just because we have thousands of young men who have accepted the Muslim religion, does not mean we have to sit by and let it continue to fester, this book will move you and equip you with the confidence we need to reach the world for Christ.

Bishop Mark C. Tolbert DD
Sr. Pastor Christ Temple Church
Kansas City, Mo

WHO IS EVANGELIST JEREMIAH CUMMINGS?

LISTEN AND SEE

I was born to a 15 year old young girl in Augusta, GA and was a product of a family that seemingly produced preachers and men who loved the Lord. I was supposed to have been an aborted child, but the turpentine and Gin had no affect on me in the womb. I ended up being raised by my grandmother, Ms. Florence Whigham, at 1513 Bleakley Street in Augusta, GA. My passion as a child was music. I loved Elvis Presley, James Brown, and Little Richard. I later moved to Washington, D.C., where I would be exposed to talent shows as early as elementary school. My fifth grade music teacher, Mrs. Davis, was the first to notice that I had a voice and encouraged me to sing at many of the school's assembly programs. I grew up listening to the Temptations and the Motown sound and eventually formed a group and called them the Sounds of Love. We went on to win the Howard Theatre Talent Show in 1969. The Sounds of Love rehearsed 8 hours a day, even on Sundays, and nobody missed practice.

In 1973, I met Harold Melvin who had a management company in Philadelphia. He eventually signed my group to a five-year contract. About a year later, Harold took me from the Sounds of Love, now called the Internationals, and made me the first tenor for Harold Melvin and the Blue Notes. My first album went gold and is now platinum. For nearly nine years I traveled around the world four times and did all the things I had dreamed about as a child, including meeting the Temptations, Stevie Wonder, and all the stars I use to watch on television.

I also at that time met a group called Kool and the Gang who where all members of the Nation of Islam, and I was intrigued at their discipline and cleanliness. I later found out that all of the members of our band were also Muslims, and I began to spend a lot of time around them and even ate with them. One night while performing in Miami, Florida, we were visited by Joe Tex, whose Muslim name was Yusef Haazes, and who was also a minister of the Nation of Islam. He would have me sit at his table after the show and would tell me that a man called the Honorable Elijah Muhammad knew of me and that Mr. Muhammad had also seen me on the album cover To Be True wearing a bow-tie. The bow tie at that time was the

dress of the men of the Nation of Islam. I
was later invited to the Sunday service by
Minister Haazes and fell in love with the
teachings of the Honorable Elijah
Muhammad.

Thirteen years later, I met the man who
reminded me of the father I never had. His
name was Minister Louis Farrakhan, the
now leader of the Nation of Islam. The day
we met we became like glue. I often wonder
why no one from the Christian church ever
had this effect on me as a young man and
why I never had a witness from the Christian
church back then. I guess you can say the
Lord wanted me to experience all of this
knowledge of the Koran and the Bible so
that I could do what I am doing now. For
nine and one half years I would dine and
ride in the cars owned by Minster Farrakhan
and I loved that man like a man would love
his own father who birthed him into the
world.

But after nine years I began to feel
emptiness in my life that I just could not
explain. So one night in 1996, I started
seeking the character of Jesus. I began what
would be 13 months of intense study for
eight and nine hours a day. I then began a
fast, because I knew from the teachings of

the Nation of Islam the benefits of fasting that thought traveled faster to the brain when there is no food to interfere with its movement. Food slows down the thought process. The fast causes oxygen to go to the brain faster. Therefore, thought is shaper. The fast would last for 43 days and on the 43rd day, the Lord visited me and filled me with the Holy Ghost. It took me 3 or 4 days to come down from that experience enough that I could write a letter to Minster Farrakhan and ask him to accept my resignation. When I tell you that he would not accept my resignation it is not to make me look like I was someone special. The only thing that bothered me about him not excepting my resignation was I knew he was hurt. But I knew also he would get over it because I know him very well.

Do I think Minister Farrakhan will accept Christ as his Lord and Savior? This is January 3, 2006, and I have heard already that Minister Farrakhan has accepted Jesus as his personal savior. The principles of Christianity were somewhat noticeable even while I walked with him in the Nation of Islam. When will he announce his change? I don't know but I can see the change. I have traveled through many religious circles and denominations since 1997. I have seen folks who have been in church all their lives, and some of them need to see and experience some street life because some of them know nothing about a man's word being his bond. I have seen egos in Bishops and Ministers that reflect a pimp-like spirit in them. I have seen also great men of God and great women of God who really try to live up to their calling. But again, I have seen selfishness that is sickening.

How can we reach the world with some who only think of themselves? How can we reach the world when in many cities there is petty jealousy between so-called leadership? How can we reach the world when some of us can't even return a phone call when we say we will? What kind of mind is this? I decree in 2006 this will have to change.

Now the Worldwide International Campaign for Christ is beginning to reach into Syria, Egypt, Jordan, Iraq and West Africa and is beginning to get the attention of the Seed of Ishmael the Muslim world. I know the Lord has Ministers and Bishops with a heart to help us reach these souls. This book, *Reaching for the World*, has grown since it was first written in 2004, and every Christian should learn what is in it, and every Muslim should read what is in it.

Maybe with the help of the Lord we will one day build a bridge to brotherhood and there will be one Lord and one faith and one baptism for all nations.

Reaching For the World

By

Evangelist Jeremiah Cummings

There appears to be a great void in the United States when it comes to understanding the knowledge of The Koran, the Islamic guide for more than one billion Muslims. As many of you may know, I am a former Muslim minister that almighty God decided to convert after 13 months of intensive study of the Bible and the Koran. The Koran is 95 percent Torah and the Gospel. A whole chapter is dedicated to Mary, and Jesus is mentioned more than Muhammad. Even the church is referred to as the people of the gospel in chapter 5:47, "And let the people of the gospel be the judge of those things we have written."

The Koran says that the people of the gospel are to judge and confirm those things written in it. Well, I have much to say about what is written in the Koran, and I have a message for one billion Muslims about many scriptures written in their Koran. I have so much to reveal to the church and how we can, as the scriptures say in Acts, turn the world upside down. I recently taught two seminars in Corpus Christi, Texas and I wish I had them ready for television, but they were not taped.

Listen to what Muhammad wrote in chapter 2:135: "And they say become Jews or Christians, and you will be on the right path. Say no, we follow Abraham the upright one." This is not at all in line with what the Koran says the Muslims believe. The Muslims confess that they believe in the Torah and the Gospel. Therefore we must let the readers of the Koran know that someone did not read Genesis 14:13, which says, "And there came one that had escaped and told Abram the Hebrew." Abraham was Hebrew, not Muslim, but the Muslims say they follow Abram the upright one.

In Isaiah 55:5 the Bible says,
> "Behold, thou shalt call a nation that thou knowest not and nations that knew you not shall run unto you because of the Lord thy God and for the Holy one of Israel."

I believe that this scripture prophetically pointed to us calling the Islamic world into account for the things written that are totally contrary to the books (the Torah and the Gospel) which they say they believe and follow. There are some scriptures that I feel are very important for the Muslims to recognize that will enlighten them as to who Jesus the Christ really is.

One of the biggest denials of the Islamic world is the divinity of Christ. The Muslims say that God could not and did not have a Son. Just to kill that statement the question is, whose son was Adam? Adam was the son of God. Almighty God formed Adam without the assistance of a woman or a man. If I can show the Muslim world the virgin and the birth of Christ in the Koran, then there should be no argument about whom Christ is. Now once I show this to the Muslim world, many of their leaders will get together and try to say that this does not mean what Minister Jeremiah Cummings says it means. They will say, he is not an Arab, or he does not speak Arabic. But they don't have the Holy Ghost either, and it is the Holy Ghost in those who know Christ who will lead all to truth.

It was Jesus who said, "And ye shall know the truth, and the truth shall make you free." (John 8:32) Now what is the truth? Even from the Muslim Koran it tells them of the birth of the Christ. It is found in Sura 21:91: "As for Mary who guarded her virginity and we breathed into her of our Spirit and made her and her son a sign." If the Koran says, "and we breathed into her of our inspiration," then the word "inspiration" in Arabic means "spirit." The Bible says the same thing, but it uses the word Holy Spirit. So as you can see the Koran even admits to the virgin birth of Christ. Therefore, if He is the Son of God (and He is), then God's ultimate aim for Islam was to first deliver the Nomads (Arabs) from idolatry and eventually reveal to their blind eyes that the Koran came from the Bible (or at least 95 percent of it did), and it states that Christ is the savior for the whole world.

Listen to this confession in Sura 2:136:
> "We believe in God and in that which was revealed to us, and in that which was revealed to Abraham and Ishmael, and Isaac, and Jacob, and in that which was revealed to the tribes of Israel and in that which was revealed to Moses and Jesus and in that which was revealed to the Prophets."

This opens up great dialogue with the Imams and Ayatollahs of the entire Islamic world. If the Koran says they believe in that which was revealed unto Moses and Jesus, then they would know that Moses prophesied of Jesus, and the prophets also foretold the birth of the coming Messiah for the whole world. The Koran is missing the scriptures of the prophets. Isaiah, Ezekiel, Jeremiah, and Daniel are missing from the Koran. But we, the body of Christ, have the missing link, and we have been chosen to connect the whole world by the missing link.

I woke up this morning with the question on my mind, why didn't God give the Muslim world the prophets – Isaiah, Ezekiel, Jeremiah, and Daniel – in their holy book called the Koran. The answer came back to me like this. God could not give the Muslim world the prophecies of Isaiah because those prophecies were pointing to the body of Christ concerning the deliverance of the seed of Ishmael, which is the Islamic world. It would be the body of Christ who would call a nation that they knew not (Isaiah 55:5). It would be the body of Christ who would tell the Islamic world the things that they have never been told simply because the Islamic world had never received the revelation of these prophecies. Notice now Isaiah 52:15:

> "So shall he [through the body of Christ] sprinkle many nations; the

kings shall shut their mouths at him: for that which had not been told them shall they see; and that which they had not heard shall they consider."

Now this revelation could not have been given to the Muslim world through their Koran because this revelation is speaking of this day and time about the Islamic world. It is we, the church of our Lord Jesus Christ, who would open up the understanding of the Koran and reveal that which their own eyes have not seen from their own holy book. The prophet Muhammad's job was to reform the Arabs in the area of idolatry. In the Kaaba during the time of Muhammad, the Nomads of Northern Africa worshiped more than 365 gods, and they were housed inside of the Kaaba. Muhammad taught them from Deuteronomy 6:4: "The Lord our God is one Lord." Muhammad symbolically left one God in the Kaaba to symbolize there is but one God.

I need you to help me take these messages to one billion Muslims through WICC-TV, and I wish to take these writings a little deeper the next time. In less than a year on MBC-TV, more than seven thousand former Muslims have seen our nationwide broadcast "Wake Up Everybody" and are now practicing Christianity as their way of life. What the politician does not know is that if you want to change a man or a nation that it can be done through Christ instead of by a gun. The Bible says "the weapons of our warfare are not carnal, but mighty through God" (2 Corinthians 10:4). This is where the church and pastors come into the picture. It is our responsibility to transform this world into the glory of God. The Bible speaks of us as "the light of the world" (Matthew 5:14). No one else can claim this truth but the children of God.

Let's go into the Koran and see what it says that might help us to lead the Muslim world into the knowledge of the truth. The first thing all of us must understand is that our God wants all men to be saved. This is God's will in 1 Timothy 2:4, "who will have all men to be saved and come into the knowledge of truth." The word "will" not only means it is God's will, but it also means that this is what God desires most. "All men" means just that. He wants the Muslims saved and the Hindus saved. Yes, He wants all men to be saved. So the best way to save a people who we know not a lot about is first not to be judgmental. We also must know what the Islamic world believes. The Koran says in Sura 11:37, "And make an ark under our guidance and our instructions and do not speak to me on behalf of those who are disbelievers, surely they will be drowned." This scripture tells us that even Noah is mentioned in the Koran and the Muslims bear witness that Noah was a messenger of God. And we know that Noah was a messenger of God from our Bible and that he did indeed build the ark. This was a sign of the kingdom of God, a permanent place of refuge and security, and nothing could or can destroy it.

The one thing that Muslims and Christians can also agree on is "the day of judgment" by an awesome God. In Ecclesiastes 12:14 the Bible says, "For God shall bring every work into judgment, with every secret thing, whether good or whether it be evil." Now from the Koran in chapter 51:12 it says, "They ask; when is the day of judgment?" Verse 13 says, "It is a day when they are tried at the fire." Continuing to verse 14: "Taste your persecution, this is your reward." If we can both understand the writing that we have from the Bible and the Koran, we then will have better insight into what has been passed down to one another.

One of the biggest problems I see between Christians and Muslims is that we have no idea what the other believes. We have Isaiah, Daniel and the prophets, but the Muslims don't. Those writings were not sent to Arabia, and I believe that this is why Jesus told us to go. But there must first be some kind of dialogue.

Let's get a clear understanding of Islam and the word Muslim. The word Islam means "submission to the will of God". The origin of the religion was neither Judaism nor Islam. The religion was simply known as The Way. When Jesus arrived into the world He announced, "I am the way" (John 14:6, emphasis added). Isaiah 40:3 states, "Prepare ye the way of the lord" (emphasis added). "And a highway shall be there, and a way, and it shall be called the way of holiness" (Isaiah 35:8, emphasis added). All men, because of rebellion and pride, have lost the way.

The Lord has given us the scriptures as a road map to guide us back to the straight way. The problem is and has always been man. Has man gone so far out of the way that he cannot turn around and avert his own destruction? The book of Proverbs says that there is a "way" that seems right unto man, but the end thereof is destruction (14:12). What I am aiming to do in the writing of this book is not only to minister truth to the Islamic world, but also to the Jews and those who have no guidance. They must come to know the reason why Jesus came to this earth and his purpose for salvation.

Did God have a plan in sending the seed of Ishmael, a reformer, in the prophet Muhammad? God made a covenant with Ishmael's seed in Genesis 17:20:

> "And as for Ishmael, I have heard thee: Behold, I have blessed him, and will make him fruitful, and will multiply him exceedingly; twelve princes shall he beget, and I will make him a great nation."

These twelve princes are all named in The Koran and there is no doubt in anyone's mind that God has made the seed of Ishmael a great nation in oil, natural resources, silver and gold. God always keeps his covenant to a thousand generations. This term, a thousand generations, simply means it is everlasting. But Genesis 17:21 is key: "But my covenant will I establish with Isaac, which Sarah shall bear unto thee at this set time in the next year." From this promised seed would come the Messiah of the world whom the Muslims call Isa.

Now the Koran declares that the Muslims believe in the Torah and the Gospel. The Torah is the first five books of the Bible. Sura 3:3 states,

"He has revealed to thee the book with truth, verifying that which came before it, and He revealed the Torah and the Gospel aforetime, a guidance for the people and He sent the Holy Spirit, that which distinguishes or discerns between truth and falsehood."

In this scripture from the Koran, the Holy Spirit is called the discrimination, but the word actually signifies the Divine Intellect or the Holy Spirit or the Discerner. Here Muhammad bears true witness that God revealed the Torah, the first five books of the Bible. But in the first five books of the Bible Jesus is concealed as Shiloh. "The scepter shall not depart from Judah, nor a lawgiver from between his feet, until Shiloh come; and unto him shall the gathering of the people be." (Genesis 49:10) It is never my aim to disrespect the Muslims, but even the Koran says that God made us of different tribes, not that we should despise one another, but that we may get to know one another. The Shiloh in this book from the Torah is a prophetic utterance of the coming Messiah, Jesus, or in Arabic, Isa. This

Shiloh came to empower us with divine knowledge and ability and to call a nation to Himself through us, the Body of Christ.

Please notice that John 10:16 states, "And other sheep I have, which are not of this fold: them also I must bring". Who are the sheep which Jesus is speaking of? Well if we go back to Isaiah 55:5, it states, "Behold, thou shalt call a nation [that] thou knowest not, and nations [that] knew not thee shall run unto thee because of the LORD thy God." I believe what the spirit of the Lord has revealed to me in this hour is that these are the descendants of Ishmael and those whom we refer to as Muslims. In Isaiah 55 the Lord says that we will call a nation whom we knew not. In Galatians 4:25 the Lord says and (the seed of Ishmael) they shall answer to Jerusalem.

Let's look at what the Bible says about the Muslim world as it relates to Christianity. In Galatians 4:22 the Bible states, "For it is written, that Abraham had two sons, the one by a bondmaid, the other by a freewoman." Notice that the Koran and the Bible are clear on the two sons of Abraham. The Muslims consider Abraham their father. They say that they believe in that which was revealed to Abraham. The Bible goes on to say in verse 23, "But he [who was] of the bondwoman was born after the flesh." This son was born because Sarah told Abraham that it was alright to have a son by her handmaiden. It was also a part of their Hebraic tradition to do so. In verse 23 it also says, "but he that was born of the freewoman was by promise." But this was still Abraham's son and God still promised to bless Ishmael and his seed, and He has done just that.

I was recently asked about the terrorists and the suicide bombers. I told the person that what you see in Israel and in the rest of the world is not true Islam, just like the Ku Klux Klan claims to be Christians but are truly terrorists. Galatians 4:24 says that these two women, Sarah and Hagar are allegories that pertain to two covenants. In verse 25, we see clearly who these covenants pertain to. For this Hagar is Mount Sinai in Arabia. Arabia is a Muslim country today and was the place of the descendants of Ishmael. Saudi Arabia is the holy capital of Islam and millions of Muslims go to Mecca, which is in Saudi Arabia, for their pilgrimage yearly. But the next few words of Galatians 4:25 say that this Mount Sinai in Arabia answers to Jerusalem.

The question I have is this: when did the call go out? The answer is now is the time. The prophecy was given in Isaiah 55:5, "Behold, thou shalt call a nation [that] thou knowest not..." Here we have a prophetic call in Isaiah and in Galatians. We have the called being told that they would answer to Jerusalem who is today the Body of Christ or the kingdom of God on earth. When this call begins to be heard, the Lord says that they will shut their mouths at our wisdom. Isaiah 52:15 states, "So shall he (we) startle many nations..." What nations? All the nations of the earth that Jesus has commanded us to take the gospel to. Now keep in mind these nations that we take the gospel to will already have a belief in some form of religion.

The prophetic promise is that we will startle many nations. Why does the Bible say they will be startled and the kings will shut their mouths at their wisdom? Why? For that which had not been told to them shall they see, and that which they have not heard shall they consider or take into counsel. That is what is happening today. God has anointed me to show the entire Nation of Islam things which they are now having to consider. It is written and since it is written it shall come to pass. Muhammad, the prophet to the

25

Arabian people and the seed of Ishmael came to them to reform them from the idolatry practiced by their forefathers. Some 365 gods were worshiped and placed in the Kaaba in Mecca, the holy place of worship for the Islamic world. Muhammad came preaching the worship of one God, Allah. The name Allah means all mighty God. The -ah at the end of the name means God in Hebrew and Arabic. The All- in the beginning of the word is self-explanatory. Muhammad was given Deuteronomy 6:4, which says "the Lord our God is one Lord" and took this knowledge to his own people. This is why time and time again in the Koran Muhammad tells his people of the Torah and the gospel and that they are the revealed books of God before the Koran.

Muhammad speaks of Jesus more than any other prophet. Muhammad even went to Luke 1:34 where there we find a conversation with the angel Gabriel and Mary the mother of Jesus. Muhammad wrote this to his own Arabian people in Sura 3:46. Mary said, "My Lord, how can I have a son and man has not yet touched me" and the angel responded, "Even so, God creates what he wills. When He decrees a matter, He only says to it be, and it is." Now Luke 1:31 reads, "And, behold, thou shalt conceive in thy womb, and bring forth a son, and shalt call his name JESUS." Let me share what Muhammad wrote in the Koran to see if there is any connection to the Bible verse I just gave you. In the Koran Sura 3:44 reads, "When the angel said; O Mary, surely God give thee good news with a word from Himself (of one) whose name is the Messiah, Jesus, your son and man has not yet touched me?" And He answers Mary stating, "Even so, God creates what he desires. When He decrees a matter He only says to it be, and it is."

Now if Muhammad could not read or write then who wrote the Koran? I was told Muhammad was illiterate and that the writing of the Koran was by miracle. How is it that when what is being revealed is 95% the Holy Bible? The Koran calls Jesus "the" Messiah, and "the" always signifies one or the only. Therefore if the Koran calls him the Messiah it is obvious to us that Jesus is more than just another prophet. In Sura 3:44 when the angel came unto Mary, he said,
> "O Mary, surely God gives thee good news with a word from himself of one whose name is the Messiah, Jesus, son of Mary, one who is worthy of praise in this world and in the

hereafter, and of those who are drawn to Himself."

As I was typing this portion of the scripture from the Koran, I noticed that here the angel did not really prophesy in the mentioning of the name of Jesus. The angel here spoke as though this Messiah has already existed by saying "His name is" instead of "His name shall be called" the Messiah, Jesus.

I want to go a little deeper. In Sura 3:47 it says, "And God will teach Him (Jesus) the book and the wisdom and the Torah and the Gospel." In the latter part of verse 48, Jesus is quoted as saying, "And I heal the blind and the leprous and raise the dead to life with God's permission." And all of this is true, but who else in the Koran did these things but Jesus. Who else healed the blind and raised the dead in the Koran. I am speaking to the Muslim world and would like to know if Muhammad raised the dead or any of the other prophets of the Koran? I know the answer but I want to hear from the scholars of the Islamic world, the seed of Ishmael, concerning what is written in these chapters and verses.

The argument today is whether the God of the Muslim world is the same God the Christians serve. And the popular thought is no. But I believe that the God of eternity had it in mind before the creation of the world to save Ishmael's seed. I don't believe that God would make a promise and declare that he has blessed Ishmael and did not have it in His mind to save Ishmael's descendants. The same God who blessed Ishmael in Genesis 17:20 is the same God that we serve today. Our God is about to turn their lives around to the point that millions of Muslims around the world, and in America, will see Jesus as the savior and the one Messiah the world has been awaiting to appear.

Listen to the Koran and its comparison to the truth of the Bible. Sura 57:3 states, "He is the First and the Last and the Ascendant (over all) and the Knower of hidden things, and He is Cognizant of all things." Now let's look at the same comparison found in the Bible in Revelation 1:8. In this scripture Jesus says, "I am the Alpha and Omega, the beginning (or the first) and the ending (or again the last)." If the Bible is 5,000 years older than the Koran, then we can see where the Koran got this truth. Why do we think Jesus spoke Aramaic? Aramaic is a combination of two languages. Notice I used the word combination. Combination means the coming together and binding of two nations. Aramaic is the Arabic and Hebrew languages combined. It is the combination of Ishmael and Isaac. It is the coming together of two nations. This is why Jesus spoke two languages combined.

I have found that it is hard for some Christians to except that God wants to save the Islamic world. There are some Christians who have a problem with my salvation even though in 14 months of this message, more than ten thousand former Muslims now call Jesus their savior. Religion has done this to the minds of some who profess to be filled with the Holy Ghost. I personally believe that they are filled with fear and insecurity.

Listen to me carefully. When God said in Genesis 17:20, "I have blessed Ishmael," God was saying that He had already set in motion the date and time of deliverance for Ishmael's seed. In this scripture, to be blessed is to be set free or delivered. This blessing also carries with it greatness and independence.

I am blessed, and if you are in Christ you are already blessed, and God has already planned your escape and deliverance from every situation and trap the devil has setup against you and me. While typing the previous paragraph at 4:30 a.m., I could not help thinking what comfort it would be for someone who is trying to escape Satan's snare this very moment. God says in Genesis 17:20, "As for Ishmael... I have blessed him." I believe and I know that God was speaking of this day and this time to bring the seed of Ishmael (the Muslim world) into the kingdom of His dear son Christ, the holy Messiah for the whole world.

Can you imagine God saving my friend Minister Louis Farrakhan and filling him with the Holy Ghost? Minister Farrakhan has already witnessed the power of God in his life because about three years ago he looked death in the face and God delivered him. Here is a man who told me at the dinner table one night that Jesus Christ is the Messiah. I am almost sure that was our last supper together before I became a Christian. But I wonder what would be the response of the Christians around the world if God brought Minister Farrakhan into the church. I wonder how many would leave the church because they would not be able to handle such a conversion. I am speaking from experience and what I am personally experiencing as a born–again believer.

Thank God He bought and built His church, because if He didn't, a lot of converts would leave or be put out by weak-minded Christians. In John 10:16 Jesus says, "And other sheep I have, which are not of this fold: them also I must bring." Then Jesus in the next few words tells us how He is going to bring them: "and they shall hear my voice." In Romans 10:17 the Bible says "faith cometh by hearing and hearing by the word of God." It is important that Muslims hear the voice of God. God will and does speak to Muslims through me from their own book. I realize that God has gifted me in this area.

God's plan will blow our minds, simply because God knows the end from the beginning and we do not. God knew in Genesis that He had already prepared the seed of Ishmael to be saved. This is why the devil is trying his best to put fear into the hearts of all people about Muslims, because you cannot be used by God if you have a negative picture of the Muslim world. And maybe that is why He saved me the way He did and how He did because I love all people of all nationalities and religions. If I did not, I would be prejudiced and that is not of God. Notice now in John 10:16 the unity and the outcome of the purpose of God allowing the other sheep who are not Christians to hear His voice: "and there shall be one fold and one shepherd." Christ is the head of His kingdom and He is calling the seed of Ishmael into His kingdom.

I was on Daystar Television Network on February 24, 2004, a day in the Nation of Islam called Savior's Day. Savior's Day is the birthday of Master Fard Muhammad, the teacher of Elijah Muhammad and founder of the Nation of Islam in the west. On this day, after 12 minutes on worldwide satellite television 3,000 now former Muslims made Jesus their Lord and Savior. They heard His voice, not mine, because it is no longer I who live, but Christ who lives in me. The life that I now live, I live it by faith in the son of God who loved me and gave Himself for me (Galatians 2:20). Listen to what and how the Koran speaks of the children of Adam. In Sura 7:27 it states, "O children of Adam, let not the devil seduce you, as he expelled your parents from the garden, pulling off from them their clothing that he might show them their shame." Now I would teach this as an allegory so that even the Muslims could see how this verse goes back to what happened in the garden in the Torah. Adam and Eve, as it states in the Koran, were expelled from the garden, and

33

the clothing Adam and Eve lost was the covering that almighty God had originally dressed them in, and that was His image and likeness.

The prophet Ezekiel calls their clothing "that which was lost." Look at Ezekiel 34:16. It states, "I will seek that which was lost, and bring again that which was driven away." This is a prophetic promise from almighty God concerning what was lost in the Garden of Eden. Adam and Eve lost the clothing of God and were expelled or put out of the garden. They simply lost the potential to grow into the image and likeness of God. Now notice Ezekiel continues to use the word "that" in this scripture. God says "and will bind up that which was broken, and will strengthen that which was sick." The reason why God now wants to save the Islamic world called the seed of Ishmael is because they never really had a chance because they were born of the flesh and not of the promise. I will get to this in a few minutes.

So now listen to how Jesus refers to that which was lost in Matthew 18:11: "For the Son of man is come to save that which was lost." Two words in this verse are important. They are "save" and "that." The word "save" carries with it the original

Hebrew thought, which means to bring man back to the starting point, or to the beginning where God originally desired for man to be. What was the original position and plan God had when he created man? It was that man would be in His image and in His likeness.

If you see someone go out into the deep part of the ocean and begin to scream for help you look for the lifeguard. The lifeguard's job is to save individuals from drowning. Now when the lifeguard dives into the water the person who is drowning is not saved yet. But, when that individual is brought back to where he or she started from, that person is saved. So it is with true salvation that you must be on your way back to where God originally wanted man to be in the beginning and that is in the image and likeness of God. Is this obtainable? Of course it is. Am I there? I'll tell you like the Apostle Paul told the Hebrews in the Bible. He said, "Not that I already obtain, but I press on toward the high calling of the Lord." (Philippians 3:14) The apostle was saying that at least he was on his way back.

Just before I resigned from my position as a leader in the Nation of Islam, I was having dinner with Minister Louis Farrakhan. He looked me straight in my eyes and said to me, "Brother, one day people will come to the Mosque and will not be able to tell the difference between the Church and the Mosque." Well I have come to ask myself, "What did Minister Farrakhan mean by such a statement?" I believe that God Himself was speaking to me through the words I heard from Minister Farrakhan's lips about what is happening in my life today. The Mosque will be transformed into a new creation (completely changed) through the understanding of the God who promised that He had blessed Ishmael (Genesis 17:20).

Again, in Genesis 17:20, "I have blessed Ishmael" means that I have already prepared a way of salvation for Ishmael in the future. And two thousand years ago, the way came in the person of Jesus Christ. Jesus said he is the Way, the Truth and the way into the life you have been waiting for. (John 14:6) If you can grasp this truth then I am asking that you say a little prayer for me as I press on toward my desire to please my Lord Jesus and as I am sent into all the world to preach the gospel of the kingdom of God.

STORIES IN THE KORAN AND BIBLE RELATE

I would like to begin to really show the relationship of the scriptures and stories in both the Koran and the Bible. I am more convinced today than I was when I published this work over a year ago that the real battle is not religion at all. But I know and realize now that the real enemy is Satan who is fighting to keep the true aim of God from coming to pass and that is the revelation of God's image and likeness in human form. In the Koran, the devil is seen as a rebellious being as a result of the fact that God said in the Koran that He was going to make a supreme ruler in the earth. The word ruler in the Koran is Raw-Daw. Raw-Daw is the Image and the Likeness of God. This word signifies supreme ruler-ship and God Himself in human form.

Listen to Sura 2:30 in the Koran: "And the Lord said to the angels, I am going to make or create a Ruler in the earth." Now watch verse 34: "And when We said to the angels, be submissive to Adam." So now notice that this ruler has the same name in the Koran as is written in the Bible. Now watch what happens next. The Koran says that they submitted, but Iblis (Satan) did not. He refused and was proud and he was one that rebelled. So we find both in the Koran and the Bible Satan rebelling over the fact that he would now have to submit to a man that God would give more authority than him and over the fact that this human being would be God's son. The fight continues until this day. It's not about religion or denominations. It's about the image and the likeness of God in human form.

This is why the Devil tried to get rid of Jesus and tried to tempt Him, just as he did with Adam and Eve. But now because of Jesus' faithfulness, Jesus was sent to bring us back to the starting point. This is the true meaning also of salvation – to bring man back to the original place that God desired for us to be before the fall of Adam.

Islam, which means "total submission to the will of God," came about through prophet Muhammad of 1400 years ago, so that he, Muhammad, could be used by God to deliver his people from the sin of idolatry.

Both the Seed of Ishmael and the Nation of Israel were in the sin of Idolatry, so God sent them a reformer to transform them from idolatry. Moses, his birth, and the instructions from God that are written in the bible are also written in the Koran. Sura 2:60: "And when Moses prayed for water for his people, we said: March on to the rock with thy staff. And afterwards there flowed from it twelve springs." This is also recorded in the bible, and in the bible there were twelve springs for the 12 tribes of Israel.

So let's see if the Nation of Israel is in the Koran. In Sura 2:47: "O children of Israel, call to mind my favor which I bestowed upon you and that I made you to excel the nations."

Let me shed some light on the interpretation of some of the Koran that many would try to misinterpret for argument. Here in Sura 2:136 the prophet Muhammad declares the Muslim's faith:

> "We Believe in Almighty God and in that which was revealed to us, and that which was revealed to Abraham, And Ishmael and Isaac and Jacob and the tribes of Israel and in that which was given to Moses and Jesus and in that which was given to the prophets from the Lord, we do not make any distinctions between any of them and to God alone do we submit."

It amazes me that most of the Muslims I meet who are not from an Islamic society think that they know what and why Muhammad wrote it like he did. First of all, it is God himself that makes a distinction about the prophets he sent. Muhammad knew whom he was dealing with 1400 years ago. He knew that he was sent to a people who were quick to worship Idols. So to keep them focused on God and God alone, he told his people that they were to make no distinction among the prophets because he knew they would begin to build images and bow down to the prophets that God sent.

We see the same thing happening in the book of Acts with Paul and Barnabas. The people declared that the gods had come down to them because they made a lame man walk. Acts 14:11: "And when the people saw what Paul had done they lifted up their voices, saying in the speech of Lycaonia, 'the gods are come down to us.'" But when Jesus went to be baptized of John the Baptist, God Himself made the distinction in saying, "this is my beloved Son in whom I am well pleased" (Matthew 3:17). It is important that, out of all of humanity getting, we get an understanding. Somebody has to teach us. I am teaching and not debating. Debates are produced by egos and are not designed to give God any glory but to bring recognition to men who claim to be scholars, but are no more than glory -seekers.

The Children of Israel in the Koran

Now let's reason together about the writing of Muhammad from Sura 2:40, because here prophet Muhammad writes about the Nation of Israel and their covenant with God.

> "O children of Israel, call to mind my favor, which I bestowed upon you and be faithful to your covenant with me.
> I shall fulfill my covenant with you.
> And Me and Me alone shall you fear."

So 1400 years ago Muhammad appears to address the Jews also. But the Jews had rejected Christ also as being born of a virgin and the Kingdom was now given to whosoever will let him come. The Nation of Israel became a shadow and a type of the future kingdom of God, which now is. In the Kingdom are those who are in Christ and these are now the seed of Abraham. You can be the natural child of Abraham and still miss the Kingdom. You must be born again from above (spiritually).

Even the rescue from Pharaoh is seen in the Koran in Sura 2:49:

"And when We delivered you from Pharaoh's people, who subjected you to severe torment, killing your sons and sparing your women, and in this was a great trial from your Lord."

All of this was written 4500 years before Muhammad was born, but it was not written to the Arabs or by an Arab prophet until 1400 years ago. I now know that God would use the similarities of the Bible and Koran to bring us to a place in time of knowing the truth. If 95% of what is written in Koran is truth from the bible then the 5% that is from the scholars can't separate the nations that God wants to make up His Kingdom. Jesus says to His disciples, "Go into all the worlds and teach all Nations." (Mark 16:14)

Next week in South Bend, Indiana, I will be blessed to reach a Middle East Television (METV) satellite that will go into 73 million homes, and another 46 million homes via DirecTV, and also another 4.3 billion homes in Asia, Australia, all of Europe and Africa. I heard from the Lord last year when He said, "When truth is on time it shall have no opposition." This is that time. As

Revelation 1 says: "For the Time is at hand."

Yesterday, after reaching all of these networks by satellite I was invited by Apostle H. Daniel Wilson to do his Kingdom broadcast in Oak Forest, Illinois. I was just telling Pastor Lawson, who serves under Apostle Wilson, how God loves to surprise his children. Once we arrived at the church, I was told by one of the producers of the program that the son of the Honorable Elijah Muhammad was a guest also on the program I was about to be a guest on. What a surprise! I had not seen or spoken to Ishmael Muhammad in eight years, and for the last two years I had been teaching about how God would redeem the seed of Ishmael and usher them into the Kingdom of God. God had set up a dialogue for a former Muslim minister who is reaching for the seed of Ishmael with the son of the founder of the Nation of Islam in the west on a nation wide broadcast. How awesome is that! I advise you to order this broadcast and witness the presence of God and prophecy being fulfilled. I later found out that day that the Shekinah Glory Mass Choir from Kingdom Valley International had performed at the Mosque before Minster Louis Farrakhan had spoken three weeks prior to this taping of this telecast. That is not the way it was when I was there. And I was told that the choir sang "Praise is What I Do," and the Muslim sisters where crying, and the Christians were shouting the name of Jesus. I would have loved to witness this historical event.

What is God doing? He is fulfilling His covenant. I have often said that 99% of the Christians in America do not know what Muslims believe simply because they have never been one, nor have they studied enough to know. We only know what others who also really don't know tell us. I have drunk form both cups for the last 31 years, and I had no idea in my head that God was preparing me to teach in this manner. I was just reading from John 12:31, and I believe that we are in the time that Jesus spoke of 2005 years Ago. Listen to what Jesus said: "Now is the judgment of this world. Now shall the prince of this world be cast out." What are you saying? I believe that falsehood is being judged and that falsehood is being cast out in this hour. I believe that this is why the Lord raised me up and is raising me up in this hour for such a time as this.

There are many who did not want black people to know the truth about Jesus and come to salvation, and I found that to be very demonic. Whenever one race of people gets angry at another race of people because they don't think that they are as human, it is sick. But in this world we still have this sickness among us. It was Satan who thought that he was better than Adam in the Bible and the Koran, and it was Satan who even thought that he was greater than God. There are Muslim scholars that know that Islam has been looked upon as a pagan religion, but many in the time of Muhammad did not want them to come into the knowledge of the truth.

I want to say that I am on the side of truth, and Jesus is the Truth. I am not on the side of theology or man's opinion of the truth. The Koran in Sura 2:105 states,

> "It is never the wish of those without faith among the people of the book, or of the pagans that anything good should come down to you from your Lord. But God will choose for His special mercy whom He will for God is full of grace abounding."

Here Muhammad 1400 years ago acknowledged that there were some who would have rather the Arabs remained in idolatry and go to hell than for them to come away from idolatry to find a greater truth. It's still like that today. There are many in America who would leave the church when minister Farrakhan gets saved. They will treat him just like the unbelievers treated the Apostle Paul and will refuse to believe that he is really changed. The bible says if any man be in Christ he is a new creature and old things (thoughts and mind sets) pass away and behold all things become new. (2 Corinthians 5:17)

I remember one night I preached at a church in Apopka, Florida and afterwards I came down into the midst of the congregation. I have around my neck a gold chain with the initial JC in gold and diamonds. The JC in gold and diamonds was the melt down of a ring I use to wear when I was a Muslim. But because I was made new I decided not to throw the ring away but to melt this 18 carat gold ring down and turn it into something that would represent the initials of Jesus Christ and at the same time also reflected the initials of my name Jeremiah Cummings. But when I stepped down to go where the congregation was my initials slipped out of my shirt between the buttons on my shirt and a sister saw it. She went to the pastor and assistant pastor of the church and told them that I was wearing a Muslim sign around my neck and she told them that I had not changed. She said if I had changed, I would not be wearing that sign around my neck. The Pastor called me at home and told me what was being said and that he wanted me to come back and confront this sister and now her husband face to face to show them what they thought they saw. By this time the whole church was suspicious. I told the Pastor that I have my initials around my neck and would be glad to come and show them what they saw. I went to his Wednesday night bible class and the Pastor asked her to repeat to me what she had told him and his wife and most of the church what she saw. She got through explaining to me that she worked in Muslim countries for five years and that she knows all of the Muslim signs and she saw on around my neck. I unbuttoned two of my buttons on my shirt and pulled out my initials and I asked her, "Is this what you saw?" After she said yes and saw that it was JC, do you think she said she was sorry? I don't even want to answer that because you know the answer. But this is the mindset of many who say that they are in the faith. But I must say also that there are some fired up people of faith that are excited about what God has done and what God is doing in the life of thousands of Muslims who are now leaning towards Jesus as their Lord.

The Bible From Genesis to Revelation in Arabic

I want to share with you an incredible incident that has occurred in my life in the last two months. By now you should know that I have a passion for truth and the salvation of the Muslim world called the seed of Ishmael in the bible. While preaching in Ft. Worth, Texas in July, I met a sister I had not seen in almost 10 years. This dear sister came up to my table and told me that she had the bible in the Arabic language. I had to ask her to repeat what she said a second time because the first time I thought she said that she had the bible in the Arabic language. So she went on to answer my request and at the end of those few words she said I can get you as many as you need; she knew I had need of them. The awesome thing about this is that the night before I had received an invitation from Pastor Shatqat of Pakistan to come and preach in his country (which he said was 97% Islamic), and now the next morning I am being handed a bible in the Arabic language.

So now I am in touch with the American
Bible Society in Lebanon, which is also a
Muslim country, about the distribution of
bible in Arabic in the Middle East. At the
same time Pastor Shatqat has contacted
pastors in Jordan, Egypt, and Iraq about
shipping these bibles as an evangelistic tool.

How did Islam grow in America from the
70's to now? It was not because the Arabs
were evangelizing this country. No it was
because the kings and wealthy leaders in the
Middle East shipped over 300,000 Koran
into America free and our relatives including
myself got ahold of them and read them
without understanding. Now God is about
to reverse the script.

It is now my desire to find the money and
the people who can truly understand what I
am saying. I am believing God for
1,000,000 bibles to be shipped over the
oceans into the Middle East, and God will
take it from there or from here to there.

The Lord has already forecasted the
Muslims coming into His Kingdom and
giving him praise in the latter day. Look
over at Isaiah 19:19: "In that day shall there
be an altar to the Lord in the land of Egypt,

and a pillar at the border thereof to the Lord." This is a prophetic promise about and pointing to this present apostolic age. Egypt is 17% Christian and 83% Islamic. So in other words, this is a description of the Kingdom of God, which is allegorically seen as a mustard seed that grows and becomes greater and taller than any tree of the forest. The 17% Christian population is a seed in the Middle East, but we from America must water that seed so that its roots can grow and consume the other 83% called the Seed of Ishmael. Hagar was Egyptian and returned to Egypt from Abraham's house. Islam had its beginning or its roots in Egypt. Its roots were the worship of idols. Israel had the same problem in the time of Jeremiah the prophet, and this was the reason why they were captives in Babylon. I have heard and read recently that the Muslims' god Allah was the name of the moon god worshiped in ancient Babylon and that this Allah is a false god. As I have explained in previous writings the name Allah means Almighty God. All is in the word itself and the Ah is God in Hebrew and Arabic. Jesus spoke what is called Aramaic which is the combination of Arabic and Hebrew.

All Nations Have Worshipped Idol Gods

According to the word of God, all nations
have made gods of worship. God in his
infinite wisdom guides man and allows man
to fall on his face and then raises man up so
that man would see that that which he
thought was god was no god. Listen to
Jeremiah 2:11, 13:

> "Has a nation changed their gods,
> which is no gods? But my people
> have changed their glory for that
> which does not profit... For my
> people have committed two evils;
> they have forsaken me the fountain of
> living waters, and hewed them out
> cisterns, broken cisterns, that can hold
> no water."

This scripture is speaking of the Nations of
Israel. We know that before God called
Abraham out from among his kindred
Abraham's father and kindred were into the
worship of Idols. We were all Gentiles in
the flesh. Gentiles are not a race of people.
Gentile is the condition of the spirit. A
Gentile is one who does not know the true
God. I will come back to this in a moment,
but I want us to see 2 Kings 17:29.
"Howbeit every nation made gods of their
own and put them in houses of the High
Places which the Samaritans had built; every

nation in the cities they dwelt." The Bible tells us the past as well as the future of generations to come. In the Bible we have two sons of Abraham, Ishmael and Isaac, and both of these nations produced generations that fell into Idolatry. Even until this day, all nations have made gods of their own, including the United States. For in this country dwells these two seeds. This is why Christ came.

Christ came to bring humanity back to the place that Almighty God intended from the beginning, and that is in His image and his likeness. War is not the solution, for you can never fight fire with fire. You must fight fire with the truth that comes from Living Waters. It was Truth that brought me from the ranks of Islam to God's Kingdom. It was the character of Jesus that made me see how much I needed him and the potential I have because of the Spirit of God that dwells inside of me.

In Jerusalem today we have the remnants of Ishmael and Isaac living within the same borders and fighting each other over a senseless matter. Ishmael says that the land of Palestine is his and Isaac says that Jerusalem is his, when in fact the earth is the Lord's and the fullness thereof the world and they that dwell in it. (Psalm 24:1) It is the same thing we have seen in the urban communities of the United States with the Crips and the Bloods who for years have been fighting over territories that neither of them own.

I am going to open up more on the Koran and the Bible, but first let's see through the eyes of God through His word concerning every nation and the everlasting gospel.

"And I saw another angel fly in the midst of heaven having the everlasting gospel to preach to them that dwell on the earth, and every nation, (note every nation on the face of the earth) and kindred, and tongue, and people, saying with a loud voice, Fear God, and give glory to Him; for the hour of his judgment is come; and worship him that made heaven and earth, and the sea, and the fountains of waters." Revelation 14:6,7

God gave the prophet John a glimpse of our day and time. In the word evangelist we find the word angel. An angel is the messenger of God. Therefore, this angel or messenger flies not in the air without a vehicle but this angel or messenger is flying on an airplane carrying the everlasting gospel to all nations, kindred, and tongues and people. I see this as myself and others who are also partakers of this calling. Jesus commissions us to go into all the world and teach all nations baptizing them in the name of the Father and the Son and the Holy Ghost. (Matthew 28:19) Think over that.

Cain and Abel in the Koran from the Bible

How did the story of Cain and Abel get into the Koran when it was foretold almost 4500 years before Muhammad was born? The truth is since most of the Muslim world has never seen or read the Bible, they think that Prophet Muhammad was the only one who ever received this revelation. This is the hour that God is using us to wake up nations and to bring the seed of Abraham into the knowledge of the true Truth. Sura 5:27 reads,

> "And relate to them with truth the story of the two sons of Adam, when they offered an offering, but it was only accepted of one of them (Abel) and was not accepted of the other (Cain) Cain said I will certainly kill thee."

We know as Christians that this story is true and we know it was written in Genesis

chapter 4. But again, the Muslim world has
no idea where this scripture originated. This
is why we must get the Arabic written Bible
into the Middle East as they did in 1970
with the Koran into America. Jesus said that
man shall not live by bread alone but by
every word that procedeth out of the mouth
of God. (Matthew 4:4) How close is the
Sura from the Koran to the truth of the
Bible? Very close, if not exact. At least
close enough to come to some common
ground about the Bible and the Koran.

Joshua and Caleb Also Found in the Koran

The story of Joshua and Caleb is also found
in the Koran as it is in the bible. The
footnotes of the Koran from Sura 5:21-26
quotes Numbers 14:1-4. The Koran shows
Moses telling the children of Israel in Sura:
5:21, "O my people enter into the holy land
which Allah (God) has prescribed for you
and turn not on your backs, for then you will
turn back losers." d Joshua the son of Nun
and Caleb the son of Jephunneh spoke unto
all the company of the children of Israel,
saying "If the Lord delights in us, then He
will bring us into the land and give it us."
The reason why he told them not to turn

back in Sura 5:21 was because Moses knew that giants were in the land. Notice the next verse from the Koran and you will see it for yourself in Sura: 5:22: "They answered and said unto Moses, in this land is a powerful people and we shall not enter into it until they (the Giants) go out from it, then surely we will go in once they leave out."

The next verse, 23, speaks of Joshua and Caleb. Two men of those who feared the Lord and had the favor of God on them said unto the children of Israel, "Enter upon them by the gate, for when you enter it you will surely be victorious and put your trust in Allah (God) if you are believers." But, we know that the Children of Israel refuse to enter into the land and I am informed that what was a three day journey became a forty year stay in the wilderness. The Koran covers the forty years like this in the same Sura 5:26 because they refused to go and possess the land. The Koran says that Moses said unto them, "It will surely be forbidden to them forty years and they shall wonder about in the land. So grieve not for the transgressing people."

The Koran and the bible are so closely related and yet so misunderstood by those of us who have never taken the time to look into them that it is difficult to see how they can be used to lead a nation of 1.2 billion Muslims, the Seed of Ishmael, into the Kingdom of God. But I thank God for not allowing me to be the aborted child that I was supposed to have been 54 years ago, for today he has opened my eyes so that I can help open your eyes.

We Are the People of the Gospel Mentioned in the Koran

The bible says "in all of thy getting get an understanding." (Proverbs 4:4) The Muslim, world, first of all, has not read the bible. In addition, although many have read the Koran, they have done so without understanding. It is like the Ethiopian eunuch in the bible who was reading from Isaiah about Jesus but needed a guide to help him understand what he was reading. The Koran speaks of the People of the Gospel and it must be understood that the People of the gospel are not the people of the book also mentioned in the Koran. Muhammad of 1400 years ago had a problem with the people of the book because many of them opposed the Seed of Ishmael along with the Roman Catholic Church. But, the People of the Gospel were those groups of Christians who lived the apostolic faith and had the Pentecostal experience. So, Muhammad tells them this in Sura 5:47: "And let the People of the Gospel be the judge of that which Allah (God) has reveal therein (in the Koran)."

Muhammad so admired the People of the Gospel. He said to them, investigate this Koran and if it does not line up with what has been revealed through the prophets then correct it and show it to us. And here we are 1400 years later and we have no idea of our responsibility to the Seed of Ishmael. So the bible speaks to Christians; it says, when we ought to be teachers we have need of one to teach us. Muhammad even calls the bible a guardian over the Koran. Listen in Sura 5:48, "We have revealed to you the Book with the truth, verifying or confirming that (the Bible) which came before it (theKoran) and a Guardian over it." The Koran says that the bible is a guardian over it. In other words, the bible is the authority over the Koran and this is a major truth that all should know.

Salvation for the Seed of Ishmael

From Genesis to Revelation, God has in many places declared salvation for the Seed of Ishmael. The Lord did not miss anybody, especially not the Seed of Ishmael. We should consider the fact that Hagar was an Egyptian woman, and it was Hagar who fled to Egypt after being put out of Abraham's house. The prophet Isaiah declared a prophetic promise concerning the salvation of the allegorical Egypt in Isaiah 19:19: "In that day shall there be an altar to the Lord in the land of Egypt and a pillar at the border thereof to the Lord." Here Egypt is allegorical of the Nations of Islam and the Seed of Ishmael. This was and is a prophetic promise pointing to this apostolic age.

Egypt is 83% Islamic, so it our desire to connect with the 17% in that land so that they may distribute bibles in Arabic tongue into the Middle East. Can you see what the Lord is doing? This is how we "Reach for the World." In every land there is a small remnant of believers. Isaiah the prophet said it like this: "Except the Lord had left unto us a very small remnant we should have all been like Sodom and we should have been as Gomorrah" (Isaiah. 1:9).
In the book of Isaiah 60:3 the prophet again refers to the Seed of Ishmael as the gentiles

(those who worship idols). He writes: "And the Gentiles shall come to thy light and kings to thy brightness of thy rising." The Lord is saying as I begin to raise you up as the Light of the World, eventually the Seed of Ishmael will see thy light and all the kings thy Glory. Your light is the glorious light of the Gospel. Your light is also the intellect we will acquire about the Koran, the book of guidance of the Muslim world. I now have access to 10 different versions of the Koran, praise the Lord for that.

In verse 6 of Isaiah, Chapter 60, Isaiah clearly calls these Gentile nations by name.

> "The multitude of camels shall cover thee, the dromedaries of Median and Ephah; and all they of Sheba shall come; they shall bring gold and incense; and they shall show forth the praises of the Lord."

Who is Isaiah speaking of here? Midian, Ephah and Sheba are the descendents of Ishmael. These are allegorical of the Muslims Middle East. You can go back into Genesis 25 and back to 1 Chronicles 1:28-33 and also see the Children of Ishmael. The verse in Isaiah 60 continues with the Seed of Ishmael in verse 7.

> "All the flock of Kedar shall be gathered together unto you and the

rams of Nebaioth shall minister to you, they shall come with the acceptance on mine altar and I will glorify the house of my glory."
Dearly beloved, this is a prophetic promise for this apostolic age concerning the salvation of the Seed of Ishmael.

What is the Original and Ultimate Aim of God?

Since I have been a Christian, religion at one time in my spiritual walk also most destroyed my desire to preach. This is way I boldly saw today that the Lord has no interest in your religion. The religions came about to get man back on track with his God since the fall of Adam as recorded in both the Bible and the Koran.

Man needed a reformer, so God raised up prophets to every nation. Even the Chinese had prophets. All nations had prophets, and the true prophets taught so that men could come back to God and put away their idols. There are people in America and throughout the world who would get angry with me because I may respectfully call the Muslims' prophet "Prophet Muhammad."

When you leave the religious spirit of this world and the Lord sets you free, you can say "Prophet Muhammad." I have been in circles that looked at me like I had cursed in public because I referred to a preacher as Rev. Harris.

Our whole aim should be the work of Christ on this earth and seeking to manifest the attributes of God on this earth – love, peace, forgiveness, joy, self-control, and charity. When we begin to teach and see these attributes in human form, then you will witness the Kingdom of God on this earth. The ultimate aim of God is his likeness in human form. God desire is to look at us one day and see Himself in human form. I never want to hear again that we are just poor sinners saved by grace, as though Grace is not God Himself. If God saved me, then God is in the process of making me into Himself. Salvation is a journey back to God. Back to the original place that man fell from in the Garden of Eden. Religion, when practiced past its time, becomes a tradition that stagnates the growth of the believer. Religion is a map that takes us back to God. You can have that old time religion and never see the Kingdom of God.

When you enter into the Kingdom you enter into the presence of God. That is what the story of Daniel and the three Hebrew children is all about. These personalities could not be destroyed because they were in the presence of God. Therefore, fire could not burn them because God had placed them in His presence through a promise. God promised in Isaiah 43:2, "When you walketh through the fire you shall not be burn and no weapon that is formed against you shall prosper." These words, when conceived into the mind of these men, moved them from themselves and put them into the presence of God. 2 Peter 1:4 tells us that the exceeding great and precious promises of God makes us partakers of His divine nature. That means invincible, which also means we cannot be stopped, destroyed, and if we stay focused we can never fail.

This is the ultimate aim of God for the whole of humanity. When we come to this point there is no more "devil," his time will have expired. And the devil knows it. So, his aim is to keep religions alive and keep man arrogant in his religion. This then makes man think that because someone is not of his or her denomination or religious beliefs that that person is on his or her way to hell. Here we fight over who has salvation and who doesn't have it while the whole world is going to hell. When you can speak to a hurricane and tell it to pull east and avoid your city and it does that the next day, then you are in the Kingdom of God and God's presence is working in you.

I live in a sub-division called the preserves, and we experienced our first hurricane in Orlando since we moved here from Texas in 2004. The winds blew at speeds of 105-115 miles an hour in our backyard. But, when it was all over, the only damage we had was a palm branch bent off one of our four palm trees in our yard. But outside of the preserves, just around the corner, it looked as though an atom bomb had been dropped. Trees were on top of houses and the streets were un-drivable. I could not believe my eyes. Now, as far as commanding hurricanes to move to the east, I told my wife that there were two powerful preachers in Houston, Texas. One of them I watch whenever I am home during the week and not preaching. His name is Bishop I.V. Hilliard of the New Light Church in Houston. I told her that he would pray and that the storm would go back eastward and avoid a direct hit on Houston and it happened just like that. As a matter of fact we better get ready for more storms, tornadoes, and even earthquakes. Religion is doing this in America, because religion does not conform us into God's image. Religion keeps the people dependant on the preacher instead of growing them into Christ. Religion keeps us selfish and keeps us from seeing and understanding what Jesus meant by

> "other sheep I have that are not of this fold (i.e., they do not call themselves Christians); them also I must bring, and they shall hear my voice and there shall be one fold and one shepherd."
> (John 10:16)

Who are these "other sheep"? They are the Seed of Ishmael. Today, they are called the Nations of Islam.

The Nation of Israel and the Nation of Islam

The nation of Israel and the nation of Islam are the nations that Almighty God made covenant with in the scriptures of the Bible in the beginning. Almighty God made his first covenant promise to Abraham: "and God said to Abraham through thee shall all the nations of the earth be blessed." (Genesis 22:18) Theologians today intentionally are taught to overlook Ishmael. Ishmael was circumcised with the rest of the house of Abraham. Genesis 17:23 states,

> "And Abraham took Ishmael his son, and all that were born in his house, and all that were bought with his money, every male among the men of Abraham's house; and circumcised the flesh of their foreskin in the same day."

This is the same day that God made covenant concerning Ishmael and Isaac. This was also the same day that Abraham himself was circumcised.

One of the greatest horrors of our day is to seek to curse what God has blessed. The other sheep that Jesus spoke of are the seed of Ishmael. Both nations fell into idolatry and both nations will be raised in this last day back to God. What can we do? First of all we can pray for them and for guidance. These Arabic Bibles are a hand of love for the Seed of Ishmael, and we must believe that we can send hundreds of thousands into the Muslim world. We are at the beginning of a spiritual revolution.

The Purpose of Religion

What is and what has always been the purpose of Religion? I am here in the Ohio Valley and was privileged to visit and speak at the correctional center that houses over 1500 inmates. For the first time in the chapel's history, Muslims wanted to attend this one and a half hour session. One of the first things I asked the over 300 inmates in attendance was "what was and is the purpose of religion?" Religion was not needed when God created Adam and Eve. Religion was not needed until the fall of Adam and Eve. The word religion in the original Hebrew thought means to re-align man back into rhythm with God, or to bring man back to the starting point with God.

The Muslims who attended were coming with the mind to have a confrontation, but for over an hour they were amazed and often gave me a standing ovation. Prophet Muhammad, I told them, was raised up among his people in Arabia to teach them and to reform them from the practice of idolatry. Most American Muslims are not taught this, and none of the Middle Eastern Muslims are taught this.

When I studied and practiced Islam, it was a way of teaching me respect for women and the discipline to study for hours. Islam taught me responsibility and accountability. Most of all, it taught us what unity and community was all about. It's about desiring for your brother what you desire for yourself. Satan has so corrupted religious beliefs that even today we have no idea what religion is. Once we are re-aligned with God we no longer need religion. Just like once your car has an alignment you don't have to go back the next week and get another one.

A God of Covenant who cannot Break His Promise

For nearly two years now I have been preaching a message entitled "The Power is in the Promise." When Adam and Noah aborted their potential in the Bible, I believe it was because they did not have a promise from God. It is a known fact that if we receive the promise of God or a promise from God, there is no way we cannot reap the benefits of that promise. I therefore believe that if Adam and Noah would have been given a promise like Abraham was given a promise, they would have remembered the promise and fulfilled the command of God. This is why I believe that the Seed of Ishmael will come to know

Christ as savior soon, simply because God promised it. This Seed of Ishmael is also known in the Bible as the Arabians, and we all know that Arabia is the Mecca of the Islamic world. All I am doing through the grace of God is revealing the true identity of a covenant people or a people under covenant.

2 Chronicles 17:11 says,
> "And some of the Philistines brought Jehoshaphat presents and tribute silver; and the Arabians (Seed of Ishmael) brought him flocks, seven thousand rams and seven thousand and seven hundred he goats."

Notice how much they had to bring to the king. Notice that even today they are rich in material wealth, and now God desires to bring them into spiritual wealth. You will also find the Arabians at the day of Pentecost in Acts 2:11: "Cretes and Arabians, we do hear speak in our tongues the wonderful works of God." But the job has been given to us who are in the Kingdom of God now to share the truth, and nothing but the whole truth, to a nation that God foretold would come into His Kingdom in the last days.

When I speak to Imams and even the inmates last week in West Virginia, they all are aware that it is Jesus whom they expect to return, not Muhammad and not Moses. Jesus said, "other sheep I have which are not of this fold; they also I must bring and they shall hear my voice of love, and wisdom, and power." (John 10:16) That's what will change the world. This must be done through the love of the truth and not by debate. I don't debate; I educate. There are religious folks still today trying to get me to debate Muslims, and the Lord has said no to me every time. There is enough war and hatred and lying in the world already and there is too much truth for anything else to stand in our way of reaching all nations.

David penned these words in Psalms 119:130: "The entrance of thy words gives light; it gives understanding unto the simple." Do you think that God's words only give light to the saved? God's word gave me light and God's word gave me understanding. Because God is no respecter of persons, His word will give light and is giving light to the Muslim world.

Even the Koran bears witness to the light of God's word. Sura 24:35 states, "God is the light of the Heavens and the earth; a likeness of His light is as a pillar on which is a lamp." God guides to His light whom He pleases. Why would this prophet of Islam continually use the term "God guides to His light whom He pleases"? I find these lines all through the Koran. I will open this understanding up to you who have read these lines over and over again without understanding.

There were self-righteous Christians in the day of Islamic conception that did not want Muslims to become inheritors of God's favor over 1400 years ago. This was the fight that Muhammad had with the Catholic Church and some Jews also. Therefore, he would always use the phrase "God gives favor to whom He pleases." I have heard some ignorant folks say things like the only good Muslim is a dead Muslim. But the only good human being (Muslim or whosoever) is one who understands the salvation of Jesus, who is the perfect example of human potential.

Can Terrorism be destroyed?

I would like to answer this question with truth and I hope that the eyes of your understanding be enlightened to the point that we will begin to pray more and more for peace in a worldly system that is falling head first. Terrorism is a spirit. It is the same word as evil. It cannot be destroyed with weapons of war. It will only increase. In the United States, the greatest and the wealthiest nation on earth, acts of evil and terrorism happen here every day.

Only the wisdom of God and prayer can change the world. The Bible says that wisdom is better than weapons of war. We cannot fight that which is spiritual with that which is material. So this country is involved in a war that will last forever and, if not careful, will destroy millions of innocent lives, and Satan will have a field day laughing at us who profess to be wise but are not. Most religious leaders will not speak what is really on their hearts from God because they feel they will be talked about by other leaders and be seen as anti-establishment. But if we truly followed the examples of the prophets, and the apostles, and Jesus Himself you would see that the so called establishments did not accept them either.

The lifestyle of many Christians is so corrupted that it makes it hard for any nation to take us seriously about serving God. We do so much harm to each other through religious politics and clicks. It is pathetic. I am praying for a change, and I may have to go back to fasting for long periods of time for this spiritual revival to happen for our own nation. I refuse to be selfish and think only of our nation and our people.

But like our heavenly Father I pray that all men be saved and come into the knowledge of the truth. Isaiah 60:3 says, "And the gentiles shall see your light and kings to the brightness of thy rising." Note also verse five of Isaiah 60:

> "Then thou shall see, and flow together, and thine heart shall fear and be enlarged; because the abundance of the sea shall be converted unto thee, and the wealth of the gentiles shall come unto thee."

Now see the nations that God is prophesying of in verse 13: "the glory of Lebanon shall come unto thee." Let's jump back to verse seven: "All the flocks of Kedar shall be gathered unto thee." Again back to verse six:

> "The multitudes of camels shall cover thee, the dromedaries of Median and Ephah; all they of Sheba shall come; they shall bring gold and incense and

they shall show forth the praises of the Lord."

Beloved, I don't know how this prophetic promise will be fulfilled, but these are the descendants of Ishmael mentioned here, and the prophecy says they are coming to us who are now in the kingdom and worship and reverence God.

Muhammad the Prophet of the Koran told his Followers what?

I want us to see that Muhammad was told and he himself also advised his followers to ask the Kingdom of Christ for understanding if one did not understand what he revealed from God. The truth is coming to surface in this hour. The greatest problem is Christian doctors of theology are very limited in their scope of the awesome plan of God concerning other nations. Reading from Sura 10:94:

> "But if you are in doubt as to that which We have revealed unto you, then ask those who read the book before you. Certainly the truth has come to thee from your Lord, so be not thee of the doubters."

Here we plainly see that Muhammad knew of the Bible and the people of the Bible. He tells his followers to ask those who read the book before you. Ask the witnesses who know the book. And today the Muslim world is asking us for truth but we don't hear them because too many Christian's leaders only want things and recognition.

In another Sura 5:47, Muhammad tells his followers to let the people of the gospel judge, or correct, or explain the things that has been revealed to him from his Lord. In other words, if it is not correct, then let the people of the gospel correct it or teach it the way that it should be taught. Let's read it together. Sura 5:47: "And let the people of the gospel be the judge of the things that are written therein. Let them be the judge of the things, the words, the stories, or the truth that Allah has revealed."

Jesus said to His disciples, "You are the light of the world. Let your light so shine that other men might see your good works and glorify the father who is in heaven." The Lord is saying to us today that we are the bearers of truth and if the world is going to know it we must seek to reveal it.

There are people emailing me information now on a weekly basis about the Koran and Islam and things I did not see when I first began to get revelation from God on my mission – people I have never met or spoken with but they have heard of my calling. Many have called me an apostle to the Gentiles. But to me, I am just Jeremiah Cummings, and to God be all the glory.

The Power is in the Promise

"As for Ishmael, I have blessed him and he shall become a great nation." As I stated before, there are some in the Christian faith that are as anti-Christ as anyone can be. I think most of these individuals are traditionally like this, not knowingly like this. But in spite of this, God's promises will be fore-filled. Since they were forecast then they will be fore-filled. Adam fell in the garden because Adam did not have a promise from God, and the same thing happened with Noah. But it was through Abraham that God made his covenant by promise. God told Adam, "Be fruitful and multiply and replenish the earth." And in Genesis 9:1, God told Noah the same thing. "Be fruitful and multiply and replenish the earth." But when God got to Abraham, notice God did not tell Abraham what he told Adam and Noah. The Lord said to Abraham in Genesis 17:6, "And I will make thee exceedingly fruitful and I will make nations of thee and kings shall come out of thee." Three promises in this one verse. Three is the number of understanding. The nations directly affected by this promise to Abraham are the Nations of Islam and the Nations of Israel. So when Jesus walked this earth 2000 years ago, Jesus spoke Arabic (Ishmael) and Hebrew (Isaac), which is known as Aramaic.

APPENDIX A

The historical evidence for Jesus (Yeshua) of Nazareth and his death by crucifixion

Non-Christian sources for Jesus

• Tacitus (CE 55-120), a renowned historical of ancient Rome, wrote in the latter half of the first century that 'Christus . . . was put to death by Pontius Pilate, procurator of Judea in the reign of Tiberius: but the pernicious superstition, repressed for a time, broke out again, not only through Judea, where the mischief originated, but through the city of Rome also.' (Annals 15:44).

• Suetonius writing around CE 120 tells of disturbances of the Jews at the 'instigation of Chrestus', during the time of the emperor Claudius. This could refer to Jesus, and appears to relate to the events of Acts 18:2, which took place in CE 49.

• Thallus, a secular historian writing perhaps around CE 52 refers to the death of Jesus in a discussion of the darkness over the land after his death. The original is lost, but Thallus' arguments – explaining what happened as a solar eclipse – are referred to by Julius Africanus in the early 3rd century.

• Mara Bar-Serapion, a Syrian writing after the destruction of the Temple in CE 70, mentions the earlier execution of Jesus, whom he calls a 'King'.

• The Babylonian Talmud refers to the crucifixion (calling it a hanging) of Jesus the Nazarene on the eve of the Passover. In the Talmud Jesus is also called the illegitimate son of Mary.

• The Jewish historian Josephus describes Jesus' crucifixion under Pilate in his Antiquities, written about CE 93/94. Josephus also refers to James the brother of Jesus and his execution during the time of Ananus (or Annas) the high priest.

"He has made plain to you the religion which He has enjoined upon Noah and which He has revealed unto thee, and which He enjoined upon Abraham and Moses and Jesus—to establish religion and not to be divided therein" (Sura 42:13).

I want us to note that the primary reason for the coming of a Prophet or Messenger to a fallen people like the Arabs was reformation and not to establish a superior religion that makes the cross of no importance. To do this is the spirit of anti-Christ. How can a religion that is only 1400 years old come and say to the foundation of all scriptures that if you do not practice what has been revealed unto us, you are doomed by God? It appears that all who practice the religion of Islam do not see their religion exactly like the Koran reveals it. This is why millions of Muslims do not even read the Koran, or when they read such things as "Take neither Christian nor Jews for friends for they are your enemies," many Muslims realize that many parts of the Koran are contradictory.

Notice Sura 3:84:
"And whoever seeks a religion other than Islam, it will not be accepted from him, and in the Hereafter he will be one of the losers." To whom is this scripture speaking? This scripture is speaking to the nomads in North-Roman Africa who were in deep idolatry. This scripture was a warning to them to change their ways. This scripture is not written to the New Testament saints. The Church had been established hundreds of years before Muhammad was born. This book was written to reform the seed of Ishmael, and I want you, the readers, to keep this in mind.

The Koran, in one sense of the word, implies that Jesus did not die on the Cross, but it was made to appear that they killed him on the cross. Notice Sura 4:157: "And I will give all of us the revelation of this scripture after its reading. And for their saying: We have killed the Messiah, Jesus, the son of Mary and the Messenger of God, and they killed Him not, nor did they cause His death on the cross, But He was made to appear to them as such."
Jesus Himself proclaimed in the Bible that no man could take His life from Him. Rather, He said, "I lay it down." It is true that his death on the cross was voluntary. No one killed Jesus. He gave up the Ghost so that we who believe in Him may have the right to eternal life. Many Muslims will say that Jesus did not die on the cross, but the Koran did not say that. The Koran says that they "did not cause his death on the cross." There is a difference.

This scripture does not say that Jesus did not go to the cross as the millions of Muslims say it reads. Again this scripture says, "nor did they cause His death on the cross." I say to the whole of humanity that the nails did not kill Jesus, nor did the spear in His side. The Bible says that He gave up the Ghost, and that He gave His life as a ransom, as a paid debt for the sins of all of mankind. I can shout off of this myself.

In Sura 4:171, the Koran says in one verse, "Far be it from God's glory to have a son." This is to say that Jesus was not, or could not be the Son of God. Then we should ask the Muslim world whose son was Adam. Was not Adam the Son of God? Was it impossible to create man from the dust of the earth, and breathe into Adam the breath of Life? Here is a Koran written in the 7th century seeking to deny the virgin birth which is in the writings of the Koran in Sura 21:91, and now the sonship of Christ. This is why God has chosen this time to bring a word from Himself so that the whole of the Muslim world, the Seed of Ishmael may know the truth, and the truth will make them Free.

Paul's Epistles

• Paul's epistles were written in the interval 20-30 years after Jesus' death. They are valuable historical documents, not least because they contain creedal confessions which undoubtedly date to the first few decades of the Christian community.

Paul became a believer in Jesus within a few years of Jesus' crucifixion. He writes in his first letter to the Corinthians,

"For I delivered to you first of all that which I also received: that Christ died for our sins according to the Scriptures, and that He was buried, and that He rose again on the third day according to the Scriptures, and that he was seen by Cephas (Peter), then by the twelve."

This makes clear that belief in the death of Jesus was there from the beginning of Christianity.

The four gospels

• The four gospels were written down in the period 20-60 years after Jesus' death, within living memory of the events they describe.

The events which the gospels describe for the most part took place in the full light of public scrutiny. Jesus' teaching was followed by large crowds. They were very many witnesses to the events of his life. His death was a public execution.

Manuscript evidence for the Bible and its transmission

The manuscript evidence for the Greek scriptures is overwhelming, far greater than for all other ancient texts. Over 20,000 manuscripts attest to them. While there are copying errors, as might be expected from the hand of copyists, these are almost all comparatively minor and the basic integrity of the copying process is richly supported.

Furthermore, when Western Christians studied the Hebrew Scriptures during the Renaissance, they found them to agree remarkably closely with their Greek and Latin translations which had been copied again and again over a thousand years. There were copying errors, and some other minor changes, but no significant fabrications of the stupendous scale which would be required to concoct the story of Jesus' death.

Likewise when the Dead Sea Scrolls were discovered they included Hebrew Biblical scrolls dating from before the time of Jesus. These too agreed very closely with the oldest Hebrew Masoretic manuscripts of more than a thousand years later. Again, no fabrications were found, but only evidence of remarkably faithful copying.

Conclusion: Jesus of Nazareth is a figure of history

Clearly there are events recorded in connection with Jesus' life that non-Christians will not accept, such as the miracles, the virgin birth, and the resurrection. However, what is beyond dispute is that Yeshua (Jesus) of Nazareth was a figure of history who lived, attracted a following in his life time amongst his fellow Jews, and was executed by crucifixion by the Roman authorities, after which his followers spread rapidly. Both secular and Christian sources of the period agree on this.

The primary sources for the history of Jesus' public life are the gospels. These were written down relatively soon after his death – within living memory – and we have every indication that these sources were accepted as reliable in the early Christian community, during a period when first and second hand witnesses to Jesus' life were still available.

We conclude that any statements about Isa (Jesus) in the Koran, made six centuries after Jesus' death, must be judged against the historical evidence from these first century sources, and not vice versa.

Further reading: The Jesus I never knew, by Phillip Yancey.

To contact the author:
m.durie@linguistics.unimelb.edu.au

The author of these notes is an Anglican Minister at St. Hilary's Anglican Church Kew. He is also a senior associate of the Department of Linguistics and Applied Linguistics at the University of Melbourne, with the honorary title of Associate Professor, and was formerly head of the Department of Linguistics and Language Studies. He has written several books on the language and culture of the Acehnese, and Islamic people of Indonesia, and was elected to the Australian Academy of Humanities in 1992 for this research work. He served as a member of the Council of the Academy for a term during the 1990's.

APPENDIX B

Abraham, Father of Faith

As members of the three great Monotheistic faiths, believers in the one, true God, let us examine our common father Abraham, and his faith in the Almighty, the Creator of all.

The Koran, in Sura 37:99-108 states, 'He [Abraham] said: "I will take refuge with my Lord; He will give me guidance. Lord, grant me a righteous son." We gave him news of a gentle son. And when he reached the age when he could work with him, his father said to him: "My son, I dreamt that I was sacrificing you. Tell me what you think." He replied: "Father, do as you are bidden. God willing, you shall find me steadfast." And when they had both submitted to God's will, and Abraham had laid down his son prostrate upon his face. We called out to him, saying: "Abraham, you have fulfilled your vision." Thus do we reward the righteous. That was indeed a bitter test. We ransomed his son with a noble sacrifice and bestowed on him the praise of later generations. "Peace be on Abraham!" Thus do we reward the righteous.' (The Koran, translation by N.J. Dawood)

And in 2:139-140 we read:

'Say [To People of the Book]: "Would you dispute with us about God, who is our Lord and your Lord? We shall both be judged by our works. To Him alone we are devoted. Do you claim that Abraham, Ishmael, Isaac, Jacob, and the tribes, were all Jews or Christians?" Say: "Who knows better, you or God?"

These verses identify the Koran's position on Abraham and his relationship with God. They can be further summarized into three essential points:

1. The author states that he will reward the righteous for their devotion, obedience and good works, based on Abraham's example. 'Thus shall we reward the righteous.' In other words, righteous works merit reward.

2. The author states that Abraham did not profess the faith known as Judaism, nor Christianity, and believers (Muslims) are to ask the People of the Book to examine whether or not Abraham, Isaac etc., were Jews or Christians.

3. Both 'Believers' (Muslims) and 'People of the Book' (Jews and Christians are people of the same God, and of the spiritual lineage of Abraham.)

It is necessary here once again, to examine the Koran's opinion of the scriptures contained in 'The Book' which Christians and Jews possessed in about 650 AD when the Koran referenced them. Sura 6:89-91 reads, (speaking about Job, Noah, Isaac, Jacob, Moses, Joseph, David, Solomon, John, Jesus etc.),

'Such is God's guidance; He bestows it on whom He pleases of His servants. Had they served other gods besides Him, their labours would have been vain indeed. On those men we bestowed the Scriptures, wisdom, and prophet-hood. If these are denied by this generation, We will entrust them to others who will not deny them.'

It is clear that what constituted scripture in the time of the Koran (and indeed does today), was accepted as previous revelation from God. What then does previous scripture say about Abraham?

First, consider this story:
Suppose you received a speeding ticket one day on the local highway. In court, you stand before the judge, and look for something to say. What would or could you say? Would you waste your time telling him that you've driven that particular stretch of

highway within the speed limit more often than you have exceeding it? Would he let you off under the theory that your 'good deeds outweigh the bad'? You know that this is the case for virtually all of the people who use that stretch of road. They usually drive within the limit except when they are late, or at least justify to themselves reason for exceeding the limit. So would this work with the judge? How much less would it work with God?

Would you then tell him that if he lets you off this time you will never break the law again? You know that this doesn't hold water. He gives you a look of, "Are you serious?" For if you actually do manage to go without breaking the law again, you're only doing what the law requires. You aren't getting extra merit or credit for doing what you are supposed to be doing anyway, and therefore, you certainly aren't removing from yourself the 'guiltiness' of speeding in the past.

Let us then look to the Torah to find what is recorded of our forefather.
Representatively, one can look at Abra(ha)m's story in Genesis as a cyclical one which centers in organization around the expulsion and saving of Hagar and her son

Ishmael. Though the actual analysis of why this is so is beyond the scope of this article, one can reference Galatians 4:21-31 for the beginnings of insight into that matter.

The following is an illustration of Abra(ha)m's life as recorded in Genesis. Information in square brackets is information which does not follow the precise observed pattern.

A Genealogical frame (11:10-32)
  B Migration from Haran; separation from Nahor   ([12:1-3]) 12:4-5a)
      C Building of altars; land promised (12:5b-9   [13.14-18])
          D Wife/Sister episode (12:10-20)
              E Border agreement with Lot (13:1-13)
                  F Sodom episode and rescue of Lot   (14.1-24)
                      G Covenant of sacrifice
                          (15: 1-21)
                              X Expulsion and rescue of

Hagar (16.1-16)

G' Covenant of circumcision (17.1-27)

F' Sodom episode and rescue of Lot (18: 1-19:38)

[E' Border agreement with Abimelech (21.22-34)]

D' Wife/Sister episode (20: 1-18)

C' Building of altar (22:6); land secured (22:17b; 23:1-20)

B' Migration to Haran; reunification with Nahor's line (24:1-67)

A' Genealogical framework ([22:20-24] 25: 1-18)

To be more concise, in another way, let us examine which parts of Abraham's life more directly relate to the Koranic quotes earlier. In Genesis 12, we see Abram leave the land of his father, and venture on the word and command of the Lord, to '. . . a land that I will show you' (12:1 all verses NKJV unless otherwise noted). God here begins to relate to Abram the special position he will have in terms of God's plan for the world. In 12:2, we read, 'I will make you a great nation; I will bless you and make your name great; And you shall be a blessing.' Then, in verse 7 we read, 'To your descendants I will give this land.' The Lord, when Abram was finally in Canaan, speaks to him in chapter 13, verse 15, 'for all the land which you see I give to you and your descendants forever.' After this (as indicated in the above illustration), Abram rescues Lot the first time, and God makes a covenant with Abram.

In Genesis Chapter 15 and in Genesis Chapter 22 there are two major areas of interest in terms of the difference between the Muslim and Christian perceptions of Abram's relation to God. Genesis 15 is the first of two major areas of interest in terms of this difference between the Muslim and Christian perceptions of Abram's relation to God.

Chapter 15:1-6 'After these things the word of the LORD came to Abram in a vision, saying, "Do not be afraid, Abram. I am your shield. Your reward shall be very great." (1) But Abram said, "Lord God, what will you give me, seeing I go childless, and the heir of my house is Eliezer of Damascus?" Then Abram said, "Look, You have given me no offspring; indeed one born in my house is my heir!" And behold, the word of the LORD came to him, saying, "This one shall not be your heir, but one who will come from your own body shall be your heir." Then He brought him outside and said, "Look now toward heaven, and count the stars if you are able to number them." And he said to him, " So shall your descendants be." And he believed in the Lord, and He accounted it to him for righteousness.'

Here, there are a number of issues that must be addressed. First, the Lord promises Abram reward, before Abram has done any work or obedience such as spoken in Koran Sura 37:108, which its author indicates is the reason for reward. God in his Wisdom and Grace has set Abram apart here, because he has believed in the only LORD. God 'accounted' Abram as righteous, not because he had yet gone to sacrifice his son Isaac, but because he had faith, evidenced by his following the voice of the LORD to leave his homeland to receive the promised land. There is a very distinct difference here between the faith and works of Abraham (and man) as justification. I will comment on this again, at the close of this article.

After this, Abram received many things, such as his name being changed from 'exalted father' in Abram, to 'father of a multitude' in Abraham, and the birth of Ishmael, and the promise of Isaac, through whom Abraham's descendants would receive an everlasting eternal covenant. The Lord established the covenant of circumcision, Sodom and Gomorrah are destroyed, Hagar and Ishmael leave, and Isaac is born.

Genesis chapter 22 is the location of the second significant (in terms of this analysis) happening. Here is the section in particular of which I wish to speak, verses 1 through 13, and 15 through 18;

22:1 Now it came to pass after these things that God tested Abraham, and said to him, "Abraham!" And he said, "Here I am."

22:2 And He said, "Take now your son, your only Isaac, whom you love, and go to the land of Moriah, and offer him there as a burnt offering on one of the mountains of which I shall tell you."

22:3 So Abraham rose early in the morning and saddled his donkey, and took two of his young men with him, and Isaac his son; and he split the wood for the burnt offering, and arose and went to the place of which God had told him.

22:4 Then on the third day Abraham lifted his eyes and saw the place afar off.

22:5 And Abraham said to his young men, "Stay here with the donkey; the lad and I will go yonder and worship, and we will come back to you."

22:6 So Abraham took the wood of the burnt offering and laid it on Isaac his son; and he took the fire in his hand and a knife, and the two of them went together.

22:7 But Isaac spoke to Abraham his father and said, "My father!" And he said, "Here I am my son." And he said, "Look, the fire and the wood, but where is the lamb for a burnt offering?" And the two of them went together.

22:8 And Abraham said, "My son, God will provide for Himself the lamb for a burnt offering." And the two of them went together.

22:9 Then they came to the place of which God had told him. And Abraham built an altar there and placed the wood in order, and he bound Isaac his son and laid him upon the altar, upon the wood.

22:10 And Abraham stretched out his hand and took the knife to slay his son.

22:11 But the Angel of the Lord called to him from heaven and said, "Abraham, Abraham!" And he said, "Here I am."

22:12 And He said, "Do not lay your hand on the lad, or do anything to him:_for now I know that you fear God_(my emphasis), since you have not withheld your son, your only son, from Me."

22:13 Then Abraham lifted his eyes and looked, and there behind him was a ram caught in a thicket by its horns. So Abraham went and took the ram, and offered it up for a burnt offering instead of his son.

22:15 Then the Angel of the Lord called to Abraham a second time out of heaven,

22:16 and said: "By Myself I have sworn, says the Lord, because you have done this thing, and have not withheld, your only son"

22:17 "In blessing I will bless you, and in multiplying I will multiply your descendants as the stars of the heaven and as the sand which is on the seashore: and your descendants shall possess the gate of their enemies."

22:18 "In your seed all the nations of the earth be blessed, because you have obeyed my voice." (NKJV)

First, it should be noted that the same promises made here in verses 16-18, were made above in the aforementioned chapters 12, 13 and 15. Here however, the Lord states, 'By Myself I have sworn.' In other words, by the most absolute, Holy standard by which truth can be stated or gauged, Himself, God has guaranteed that these promises shall come to pass. Here,

Abraham by his faith, was given the assurance that no longer could sin or disobedience (or anything) turn the fulfillment of the promises of the Lord from him and his descendants.

Second, there is one key to understanding the entire situation of the above verses, that is verse 12, specifically the section emphasized above. '...for now I know that you fear God...' In other words, the purpose of the test was to determine through Abraham's actions, whether or not Abraham truly feared the Lord. This 'fear' is not simple trepidation of danger or the act of being scared of something, but fear in the sense of complete faith and submission. The test was not directly to get Abraham to go to the point of lifting the knife above Isaac for it's own sake, but to testify to the beliefs Abraham held, and the degree to which the Lord was his 'living, active' Lord. Third, since Abraham did not actually complete the work, the work itself for its own sake cannot be the reason for the 'reward'. I will speak of the Korans interpretation in a moment.

So, if Abraham's works did not accumulate 'rewards' for him, and those works attested to the true matter under test, namely Abraham's faith, then his faith was graced by the reception of the covenant of everlasting Lordship from the one and only God. This is the real 'reward' for Abraham's righteousness, and was not earned by the works per se, but by the faith Abram had in God, which was exemplified in his works, the fruits of his faith.

The disciples and apostles of Christ were aware of these important distinctions about Abraham, and accordingly commented on them in the books of the New Testament:

James 2:21-24 'Was not Abraham our father justified by works, when he offered his son Isaac upon the altar? You see that faith was active along with his works, and faith was completed by works, and the scripture was fulfilled which says, "Abraham believed GOD, and it was reckoned to him as righteousness"'(RSV) Romans 4:1-5 'What then shall we say about Abraham our forefather according to the flesh? For if Abraham was justified by works, he has something to boast about, but not before God. For what does the scripture say? "Abraham believed GOD, and it was reckoned to him as righteousness." Now to one who works, his wages are not reckoned as a gift, but as his due. And to one who does not work, but trusts him who justifies the ungodly, his faith reckoned as righteousness." (RSV)

Now, these two authors, James and Paul are often misquoted by Muslims, (and even some non-believers) to point to two apparently different salvation "mechanisms" in the Christian faith. However, on closer inspection, one can see that both emphasize either faith or works, but only in order to underline the requirement for both. In other words, faith in God, produces works, and faith without works is dead. So are works in vain, without faith. James states that Abraham, in performing his good works, is completing his faith. He is not working to gain merit, or reward, but to testify to his faith. In other words, to glorify God. Paul, likewise, is stating that no one can do righteous works before the Lord which surpass His (God's) in order to be able to boast. On the contrary, it is faith in God, which_evidenced through_the works and not_by_the works, receives grace from God, and this is a gift, that no man should boast. Abraham, received a reckoning of righteousness not as a reward for his works, (which the sacrifice of his son was NOT completed anyhow), but for the faith which evidenced through the binding of his son testified to. There is a real, important difference here.

Let us then reexamine the Koranic account of 37:1-2-108 above. Abraham had a vision in which he was sacrificing his son. 'Allah' states that Abraham has 'fulfilled' his vision. Now, if Abraham's vision included completing the sacrifice of Isaac, why did the author say it had been completed, when it hadn't? If the vision Abraham had included him not killing Isaac, being stopped at the last instant by the Lord, intervening to save his son, then how could this have been anything even remotely resembling a 'bitter test' deserving of a 'reward'? Knowing that the Lord would intervene and save Isaac, how could this have been a test worthy of anything? Knowing one will not lose anything save for a couple of days of their time, to inherit 'the praise of later generations' seems more than worth doing.

But further, the reward in the Koranic account is clearly attributed to Abraham's works of obedience. How is it that he was rewarded for something that was left undone? The actual 'vision' Abraham had of sacrificing his son, mentioned as fulfilled by the author, was left incomplete. Yet this is the basis of Islamic theology, as indicated in Sura 2:140 above, 'We shall both be judged by our works.' I refer again to the story mentioned at the beginning of this article. How does one by doing only what is required make up for that which we have failed in already? We can't.

It is also true that Jesus spoke of reward from God. For example, in Matthew 6:1-4 we read, 'Take heed that you do not do your charitable deeds before men, to be seen by them. Otherwise, you have no reward from your Father in heaven. Therefore when you do a charitable deed, do not sound a trumpet before you as the hypocrites do in the synagogues and in the streets, that they may have glory from men. Assuredly, I say to you, they have their reward. But when you do a charitable deed, do not let your left hand know what your right hand is doing, that your charitable deed may be in secret; and your Father who sees in secret will Himself reward you openly (2).' This seems to suggest as the Koran states, reward for good works.

However, Jesus continues on to speak in the same breaths, verses 5 and 6; 'And when you pray, you shall not be like the hypocrites. For they love to pray standing in the synagogues and on the corners of the streets that they may be seen by men. Assuredly, I say to you, they have their reward. But you, when you pray, go into your room, and when you have shut your door, pray to your Father who is in the secret place; and your Father who sees in secret will reward you openly (2).'

How does prayer merit reward, and what reward is merited by prayer, something so unique and diverse to each individual? To find the answer to this question, we turn to the original Greek, contained in the UBS4 Greek/English Interlinear Translation, and find something intriguing. The words Jesus actually used, as the 'reward' God will give us in verses 4 and 6, is 'repay you'. This differs from the literal 'reward' that the hypocrites of verses 2 and 5 seek from men. In other words, they seek as verse 2 states, 'glory' from their fellow men. So what will God repay us, and for what, as everything we have is His to begin with? The only place we actually see the word 'reward' used by Jesus here in terms of what God will give us, is in verse 1, which more accurately reads transliterated, 'But be careful the righteousness of you not to demonstrate before men with the aim to be seen by them;

otherwise, you have no reward with the Father of you in the heavens.'(UBS4)

So righteousness is that for which reward or repayment is spoken of. Righteousness evidenced in prayer and charitable works. Jesus knew exactly what God had been saying to Abraham so many centuries before.

Therefore, I would like to return once again to the statement made in the opening quote of this article, from the Koran in the same Sura 37:108, 'We called out to him, saying: "Abraham, you have fulfilled your vision." Thus do we reward the righteous.' Is this saying what Jesus said above? Though the English words 'righteous' and 'reward' appear together, are they saying the same thing?

Nahmanides, a great Jewish Rabbi and expositor on the Torah in the twelfth century, wrote in his 'Commentary on the Torah-Genesis' chapter Lech Lecha on Genesis XV:

'(Genesis, my comment) 6. And he believed in the Eternal, and he accounted it to him for righteousness. The correct interpretation appears to me to be that the verse is stating that Abraham believed in God and he considered it due to the righteousness of the Holy One, blessed be He, that He would give him a child under all circumstances, and_not because of Abram's state of righteousness and his reward_(my emphasis), even though He told him, 'Your reward shall be very great'(verse 1, my comment). Thus from now on he would no longer have to fear that sin might prevent the fulfillment of the promise. Now, although in the case of the first prophecy, Abraham had thought that the promise was conditional upon the recompense for his deeds, yet now since He promised him that he should have no fear on account of sin and that He will give him a child, he believed that the thing is established_by God_(my emphasis).

Also, one of the greatest Rabbinical Jewish mind's in history, Maimonides in his 'The Guide for the Perplexed', chapter LIII - Explanation of Hesed (Love), Mishpat (Judgement), and _Zedakah (Righteousness)_ writes: 'The term Zedakah is derived from zedek, "righteousness"; it denotes the act of giving everyone his due, and of showing kindness to every being according as it deserves. In scripture however, the expression Zedakah is not used in the first sense, and does not apply to the payment of what we owe to others. When we therefore give the hired labourer his wages, or pay a debt, we do not perform an act of Zedakah. But we do perform the act of Zedakah when we fulfill those duties toward our fellow-men which our moral conscience imposes upon us; e.g., when we heal the wound of the sufferer . . . When we walk in the way of virtue we act righteously toward our intellectual faculty, and pay what is due unto it; and because every virtue is thus Zedakah, scripture applies the term to the virtue of_faith in God_. (And not deserving retribution for works, my emphasis and comment) Comp. "And he believed in the Lord, and he accounted it to him as righteousness"(Gen. 15:6)'

In other words, the Grace of God. On the righteous, those with faith who testify by their works, God will and has poured out his grace. This is the true reward for Zedakah that Jesus knew would be poured from His hands, His feet and His side on all those who had faith like Abraham.

One can see from this material, that the possibility exists that the writer of the Koran simply misunderstood, or rather, incompletely understood the implication and literal description of Abraham's righteousness, and from this created the underlying doctrine of the Koran, that of salvation through obedience and works. There is no other way to interpret it in my opinion. Abraham, the father of our faith did not 'earn' his reward, as then he would not have been reckoned as righteous, but rather reckoned as obedient. Abraham_was_ obedient, but it was because of his faith that the Lord set him apart and named him Abraham.

The reason for this exercise, was to show that dependence on works themselves for salvation are not how our father Abraham was accounted as righteous and rewarded before the Lord. In claiming 'true submission' or otherwise, one must examine the doctrine they espouse and test it's validity against what it claims. The Koran in my opinion cannot be what it claims to be, (in part) as it calls men and women to 'save' themselves by right conduct and thought. Though these are requirements in Christianity as well, one is not directly saved by their charitable works or obedience in prayer. Jesus knew this, and so did Abraham.

Luke 7:44-50 'Then He turned to the woman and said to Simon, "Do you see this woman?

I entered your house; you gave me no water for My feet, but she has washed My feet with her tears and wiped them with the hair of her head. You gave Me no kiss, but this woman has anointed My feet with fragrant oil. Therefore I say to you, her sins, which are many, are forgiven, for she loved much. But to whom little is forgiven, the same loves little." And He said to her, "Your sins are forgiven." And those who sat at the table with Him began to say to themselves, "Who is this who even forgives sins?" Then he said to the woman, "Your faith has saved you. Go in peace."

John 8:56-58, "'Your father Abraham rejoiced to see My day, and he saw it and was glad." Then the Jews said to Him, "You are not yet fifty years old and have You seen Abraham?" Jesus said to them, "Most assuredly, I say to you, before Abraham was, I AM.'"

note 1, NKJV alternately reads, 'your exceedingly great reward'
note 2, United Bible Society (UBS) 4th edition Greek Text does not include 'openly'. Only KJV (NKJV) and NEB include this manuscript textual addition

APPENDIX C

Is Allah the God of the Bible?

In an article on the Islamic news group somebody wrote:

...It is clear from the way the passages [in the Koran] are constructed that the God making His revelation to the prophet Mohammed considers Himself to be the same God that made revelations to these other prophets. Consequently, the Allah of the Holy Koran is, in fact, the God of the Old and New Testaments.

Now, of course, if you consider one text or the other to be false, then there are two separate gods being referred to, one false, one true, But textually, the Holy Koran is directly linked (through) references to people and events to the Old and New Testaments.

Even if the Koran is not from God I would not expect anything else. Let me give you an illustration to make clear why.

Suppose you read two interviews with an important person [president of the US or whomever you fancy to imagine] in two different newspapers.

You read them closely and you find that they are mightily contradictory so that you start wondering if those statements really can come from the same source. But both claim that they had an interview with the President at the White House and that is exactly what the President told them. But taken together they just don't make sense.

You do some research and find out that one of them really had an interview. But the other journalist was denied the interview. For some reason [pressure from the newspaper: you write this interview or you are fired or any other imaginable reason] he needs this interview, and comes to the conclusion that he knows enough about the President already to be able to make one up.

But obviously he has to make it look real. So he writes as if it is real. The President will refer back to his earlier successes, his earlier interviews where he said things to point out that he kept his promises, etc., etc. Just like a real interview MIGHT have been.

It is so skillfully done, one might not even have found the fraud if there hadn't been the real interview and the two just are so much at odds that they can't both be true.

Obviously, both the real and the fake one do write about the SAME President. The difference is not the topic, not the *claimed source* of the interview, the difference is that one *is* authorized by the President and the other is not.

Yes, the Koran talks about the same God. And it obviously takes great pains to connect this same God back to what he might have said if he had given revelation. Sure, both books are talking about the same God, but the question is whether they are both from the same source. Is the God they are both talking about actually the source of both of them?

Well, Koran and Bible are very much similar in many things, just as the reporter who was denied the interview would be able from earlier sources, from good research, or even just from good common sense to make up something that would look pretty close to a real interview. But that doesn't MAKE it a real interview.

The God the Koran talks about is the same. And Muslims do worship this one and only

Creator God. The question is not whether Muslims and Christians have the same God [there is only one Creator after all], the question is if their book is FROM this God which it claims to be from. Without question: The Koran speaks ABOUT God, but is it FROM God?

The TOPIC is the same, but is the SOURCE the same? The many unresolvable contradictions would deny it.

Now, the reporter doesn't even have to be dishonest. Let me change the story a bit to accommodate it more to the situation as I think it could have been.

Let us suppose the reporter wanted an interview with the President, but then he meets somebody claiming to be the aide of the President. "The President is unavailable at this time, but I am authorized to give you any information you need," he says.
So, our reporter is glad to not have to go home with empty hands and interviews the aide who is more
than willing to give a lot of information and much of it even without being asked for it.

The reporter is honestly convinced he heard the most authentic voice of the President available to him at this time. The problem is, as one finds out later, that the person posing as the Aide of the President was a fraud. And all the reporter wrote was made up by him.

The reporter was honest, but the source was false. And obviously again, the source which is false, but interested to be taken for true will make sure that things do sound thoroughly authentic. If he would claim absolutely impossible things he would be discovered immediately.

The prime question is:

Is the Koran FROM God?

or equivalently:

Is Muhammad a prophet sent by the one and only true God?

Even though I did bring up in this article the question "If not from God, what then is the source?" This is not a question of great interest to me. If I can establish that it is not from God, I do care very little by what dynamics and means it actually came into existence. Other human information? Thoughts from Muhammad's subconscious?

Demonic influences? A mixture of those three? Yet another source? That is all quite unimportant. If it is not God, then I don't believe it and don't care much what else it is.

This posting was only to make clear that the God of the Koran and of the Bible can be the same and obviously are the same, yet nevertheless it can be true that one is true revelation while the other is not.

Muslims obviously will ask the same question about the Bible. Muslims do not believe that it is from God in the exact form as it is today [that is what corruption is all about]. Many Muslims even believe that many of the books in the Bible didn't belong in there in the first place. So, your accusation is just the same as my explanation above. You would concede that the Bible talks about the same God as the Koran, but that God is not the source of the

Bible and hence it has to have some other source.

Given that this scenario is your accusation, I hope that you Muslim reader will not be too offended when Christians do have similar thoughts about the Koran. Actually, there is no other alternative. Even if we do not clearly speak it out all the time, the consequence can only be: If it is not from God, then it is a (clever) fraud of some sort and has to have another source, well-meaning, subjectively honest maybe, but the source is something else, and it is rather irrelevant what exactly it is.

To come back though to the original question: I believe that those who say Bible and Koran speak about a different God, confuse "topic" and "source" or "topic" and "content." Because the content (description) is different one might say it is a different understanding of God. To a certain extent this justifies to say that it is a "different God."

Hearing a different description of God by Christians and Muslims, some come to the conclusion you must be talking about different entities, and that is understandable. Others come to the conclusion that the entity is the same [because there is only on Creator God - and both agree that there is only one and hence they talk about this same one] but because of the differences one of them must have false information. At least SOME false information even though much of it is the same and probably true information.

If I say "This house is painted red all over" and another says "This house is painted green all over" then there are two possibilities: Either we are talking about two different houses [two different gods] or we are indeed pointing to the same house [god] but one of us is giving wrong information.

But since *all we know about God* comes to us through some kind of "information" [written or oral], if the information is different, our (understanding of) God is different. We do worship God according to what our understanding is of him. Subjectively different understandings are different gods. If I hear of a red house within my mind independent of the real color of the house. The houses I "see" [think of] are actually different. So different information about God produces within our mind a different "god" and we do worship God according to the "god" we know about. In that sense, our gods are different. [In that sense, the "imagined gods" of the Muslims among themselves and the "imagined gods" of Christians among themselves are different since everybody does have a somehow different understanding of God.]
I hope these thoughts help some of you to organize your thoughts on this rather important question [which I have been

struggling with as well for quite a while].
Feedback is welcome.

Obviously the next step has to be the
investigation of the two "interviews" or
"revelations" for clues whether they are
indeed informed by the correct source or
whether there are evidences why one of
them is not from the true God it pretends to
originate from.

Another illustration might make even clearer
the different way people look at this
question. Think about different artists
painting a portrait of the same person. Some
artists are realists who paint all the outward
appearance detail for detail, another might
be an intimate friend of the person he
portrays and will use his knowledge of the
character of his friend to paint a picture
which is very much a true representation,
but more inspired by the inner reality than
meticulous physical details. A third one is
an abstract painter and not knowing the man
at all he might put into this picture more
about his own feelings and impressions in
regard to this person than what the person
really is.

The Bible speaks of Jesus as God's live self-
portrait given to us:

Anyone who has seen me has seen the
Father. (John 14:9)

Who, being in the very nature of God . . .
being made in human likeness. (Philippians
2:6-7)

He is the image of the invisible God . . .
(Colossians 1:15)

The Son is the radiance of God's glory and
the exact representation of his being . . .
(Hebrews 1:3)

The Biblical books then are "painted
images" of God, of Jesus, of the prophets, .
. . by people like the second painter who
paints a friend. Their deep experience and
knowledge guided in addition by the Holy
Spirit of God gives an accurate picture of the
true character. For example, we learn much
about the character of Christ in the Gospels,
but there is not one physical description of
him.

My impression is that the Koran is an image
of God like a portrait made by an abstract
painter, a person who did not really know
God intimately, but puts into this picture
much that he thinks God should be like.
Since our human reason and philosophical

118

thoughts about God are relatively similar in many ways, this picture will appeal to many people who recognize their own thoughts about God in this portrait. But it doesn't mean therefore that it is true. It would only mean that many people think similar about God and like to view him the same way.

And maybe the abstract painter has seen an old painting of the person who was damaged in many places, he had some true glimpses, but he had to fill in large parts by using his own imagination.

Similarly, Muhammad was not able to read the earlier scriptures for himself, but he had heard from the Jews and Christians a good number of stories. He had therefore some memory of the true image, he used those memories and supplied by himself the other pieces that were missing and not available to him. This hearsay accounts for a good number of similarities on the surface, but the fundamental differences come from not knowing this God by personal relationship as the Biblical writers did.

When we think about how something for somebody should look like (for example when reading a fiction book without pictures) our image of them is most often informed by our prior life experiences and might look very different from the image other people have when reading this same book, and especially different from the image the author of the book had in mind when writing it. And that holds for biographies and history books as much as for fiction.

In this sense, even though the above painter intends to paint the real person, since he is doing so without true knowledge of this, this person he will paint something that he imagines it to be and this imagination is informed by the environment he grew up in and the world view that has made him the person he is.

I think this illustration is the correct one to understand the position of Dr. Morey and others who write books like "Allah the Moon God." They seek in the society of Muhammad for clues about their images and understanding of God and then (for lack of true knowledge) this will be the source for Muhammad's teaching about God. Given the very idolatrous background of Arabia at the time of Muhammad, so the reasoning goes, Muhammad realizes that multiple gods cannot be true, but nevertheless in his attempt to get rid of all the minor gods/idols the image that Muhammad paints about (the only) God is informed by his upbringing including the understanding about the gods his society was used to, especially the highest of these idols, the moon god. Dr. Morey sees Muhammad as taking the highest of those gods and declaring him the only one and destroying the lesser ones, but retaining many of the characteristics of this highest of the idols.

I can understand the approach, but I think it is not very helpful in the dialog and debates with Muslims. It is obviously not what Muslims believe. But he doesn't say Muslims believe this. He argues that this is the source, but Muslims don't realize it.

In fact, Muslims do exactly the same thing, when they claim that the source of doctrines like "the incarnation," Jesus being "the son of God," "the Trinity" etc. are all pagan concepts brought into the church when Christianity spread from the Jews to the Gentiles. Muslims charge the Christians that they took pagan concept and "baptized them" just as Dr. Morey and others charge that Muhammad brought the character of the Arabic moon god into his preaching of monotheism.

As much as I think that this approach is unhelpful for dialog or even debate, I fail to see how the Muslims have a right to be outraged while they do the very same thing when looking at the Christian understanding of God.

The above is obviously my Christian understanding when looking at the situation. The Muslim might take this analogy and say that Muhammad didn't paint at all, but that he was handed a photograph exactly representing the heavenly original.

I might then again, accept that the preservation in great detail of the Koran could be likened to a photograph, but it is a photograph of the abstract painting above, an exact representation of an image that was not based on reality in the first place. Certainly a very careful hand copied painting of the real image will be nearer to the truth than an exact photograph of a painting that was never true. And it can be shown that both Koran and Bible have their textual variants, there is no complete preservation on both sides, yet both are very well preserved and we can be confident that the text we have today is essentially identical to the original manuscripts.

The fact that preservation says nothing about truth, and that there are books with false content which are meticulously preserved, and also knowing that both Bible and Koran can be shown to be well preserved, leads back again to the most important question:

How do we know that the book you believe in (Koran or the Bible) was originally from God and represents the true image?

APPENDIX D

Muhammad in the Bible?

Muslim Argument from Biblical Texts

The Prophet Like Moses in Deuteronomy 18

Muslim: In the original Tawraat there were clear predictions of the coming of our holy Prophet. One of them survives and is found in Deuteronomy 18:8 where Moses clearly foretells the coming of another prophet who would be just like him.

One of the great arguments raised by Muslims in discussion with Christians is their claim that Muhammad is foretold in the Bible. The issue derives from a passage in the Koran which has led Muslim scholars, from the earliest days of Islam, to search for passages in both the Old and New Testaments to prove that their Prophet's coming was indeed prophesied by the former prophets. Some of the books Muslims have written on this subject draw numerous passages from all over the Old Testament and one or two from the New but, in general conversation with Muslims, only two prominent examples are usually put forward and we will consider these in this chapter. The Koranic verse is:

Those who follow the Apostle, the unlettered Prophet, will find him mentioned in the (books) with them, in the Tawraat and the Injil. Sura 7:157

In both cases' Christians will find that there can be no doubt that the particular passages refer to Jesus and the Holy Spirit respectively.

Muslim Arguments on the Prophet "Like Unto" Moses

The first of the prophecies they claim foretells the advent of their Prophet is found in the following passage where God addressed Moses:

I will raise up for them a prophet like you from among their brethren; and I will put my words in his mouth, and he shall speak to them all that I command him. Deuteronomy 18:8

The first argument is that Muhammad must be the prophet foretold because he was like Moses in a way that none of the other prophets were. As Christians claim the prophecy refers to Jesus, Muslims argue further that they do not have to consider any other prophets but only have to bring comparisons between Moses, Jesus and Muhammad. The arguments run generally like this:

1. Moses and Muhammad led Normal Lives in Every Way

Their lives followed a perfectly normal course unlike Jesus where every feature of his life was unique or unusual. They both had a father and a mother whereas Jesus was born of a virgin-woman and had no human father. Both died normal deaths at the end of lives that went their full course whereas, according to the Bible, Jesus died tragically when he was only thirty-three. Moses and Muhammad both married, but Jesus remained a bachelor all his life. So Muhammad must be the prophet who was to come like Moses.

2. Moses and Muhammad Became the Leaders of their People

In the later years of their lives, after initially being rejected by the Jews and Arabs respectively, Moses and Muhammad became the political and religious leaders of their nations. They died as undisputed rulers whereas Jesus had only a few followers at the end of his life, having been rejected by the chief priests and the people.

3. Their Successors both Conquered the Land of Palestine

Shortly after their deaths successors to both Moses and Muhammad led armies into the land of Palestine and conquered it. Joshua conquered the land of Canaan, and it was then known, and settled the Jews in what became the land of Israel while Umar, the second Caliph after Muhammad, conquered the same land for Islam and settled Muslim Arabs in it where they are to this day. Jesus, however, was driven out of Jerusalem and put to death by the Romans who continued to rule the land for centuries to come.

Similar arguments are put forward to supposedly prove that it was Muhammad, and not Jesus, whose coming was foretold.

The Key Features of the Unique Prophet to Come

The Muslim arguments hardly touch on the key issue. Moses was a unique prophet who had been commissioned to introduce a covenant between God and the people of Israel. The prophet who would be like him would obviously have to have certain distinguishing features that would make him like Moses in a way no other prophet was. Christians can argue like Muslims that Moses and Jesus both left Egypt to fulfill their ministries which Muhammad never did. "By faith he forsook Egypt" the Bible says of Moses (Hebrews 11:27), and again "Out of Egypt have I called my Son" it says of Jesus (Matthew 2:15). What, however, were the unique features in Moses' prophethood? Let us consider them.

1. Moses was the mediator of a Covenant

In the same passage as the prophecy we are reviewing, God said to the people of Israel that he would indeed raise up for them a prophet like Moses, "just as you desired of the Lord your God at Horeb on the day of the assembly" when they had pleaded that God speak to them through a mediator only (Deuteronomy 18:16). Moses mediated a covenant between God and the people when, after the ten commandments and other laws had been delivered to them, he anointed the Book of the Law and the people with the sprinkled blood of calves and goats as well as the tabernacle and vessels used in worship, saying "This is the blood of the covenant which God commanded you" (Hebrews 9:20).

2. Moses Knew God Face-to-Face

Moses had a unique relationship with God. For forty years unabated God spoke to him directly in a way he never did with any prophet who preceded or followed him. The Bible says:

Thus the Lord used to speak to Moses face to face, as a man speaks to his friend. Exodus 33:11

The Koran confirms this unique relationship, saying "and to Moses Allah spoke directly" (Sura 4:164) in contrast with another verse where the Koran says "it is not fitting for a man that Allah should speak to him except by inspiration, or from behind a veil, or by the sending of a messenger" (Sura 42:51). We need, therefore, to look for a prophet who had a similar unique relationship.

3. Moses Performed Great Signs and Wonders

For many years Moses performed many miracles, such as the many plagues he brought down on Egypt, the dividing of the

Red Sea and the daily manna from heaven. No prophet could be said to be like Moses if he could not do the same. We have already seen that Muhammad performed no miracles during his life according to the Koran and the following charge against him by the pagan Arabs during the time of his own mission is very significant:

Why are not (signs) sent to him, like those which were sent to Moses? Sura 28:48

Simply put, the argument is that if Muhammad was indeed the great prophet he claimed to be, why was he not like Moses in the key features of his prophethood? Muhammad mediated no covenant, did not know God face-to-face (the Koran according to all Hadith records and Sura 2:97, was mediated to him solely through the angel Jibril), and performed no miracles. So he cannot be the prophet foretold in Deuteronomy 18:18. This verse, describing Moses' ministry at the end of his life, emphasizes the uniqueness of his prophethood:

And there has not arisen a prophet since in Israel like Moses, whom the Lord knew face to face, none like him for all the signs and wonders which the Lord sent him to do in the land of Egypt, to Pharaoh and to all his servants and to all his land. Deuteronomy 34:10-11

It is clear from this passage that the prophet to come who would be like Moses, would be identified at least by his close direct relationship with God and by many signs and wonders attending his ministry. That prophet could only be Jesus as we shall see in the next section.

Jesus - The Prophet Foretold by Moses

Muslim: What evidence do you have for your claim that Jesus was the prophet foretold by Moses? He was a great prophet but his mission appears to have ended in failure after just a few years. He did not share the greatness of Moses and Muhammad.

It is important, right at the start, to point out to Muslims that the Bible expressly applies the prophecy in Deuteronomy 18:18 to Jesus on two occasions. The Apostle Peter, claiming that God had foretold the coming of Jesus through all the prophets, quoted the text as proof that Moses has done so (Acts 3:22). Stephen, the early Christian martyr, also appealed to the same text as proof that

Moses was one of those who had "announced beforehand the coming of the Righteous One," Jesus, whom the Jewish leaders had now betrayed and crucified (Acts 7:37). We will proceed to see how Jesus fulfilled the three unique features we have already considered.

The Mediator of the New Covenant

Muslims occasionally argue that, according to Christian belief, Jesus was the Son of God and could not have been a prophet in the normal way. In reply there are numerous passages where Jesus called himself a prophet (e.g., Matthew 13:57) as well as the Son of God (John 10:36). Having taken human form to proclaim the Word of God just as the previous prophets had done, made him likewise a prophet in the true sense of the word. Let us now see how he was the prophet to come like Moses.

1. Jesus was also the Mediator of a Covenant

At the time of Jeremiah, many centuries after Moses' time, but long before the days of Jesus, God promised that he would make a new covenant between himself and his people. As the nation of Israel had consistently rejected his laws, he regarded the original covenant made with Moses obsolete, but promised that he would now enter into a special relationship with his own people by forgiving their sins and writing his laws on their hearts (Jeremiah 31:31-34). The New Testament declares that Jesus was the mediator of this covenant (Hebrews 9:15). To ratify the first covenant we read:

Moses took the blood and threw it on the people, and said, "Behold the blood of the covenant which to Lord has made with you in accordance with all these words." Exodus 24:8

As the first covenant had been mediated through Moses and ratified with blood, it was only to be expected that the prophet to follow like Moses would do likewise. So, just before his death on the cross, Jesus said:

This cup is the new covenant in my blood. Do this as often as you drink it in remembrance of me. 1 Corinthians 11:25

2. Jesus also Knew God Face-to-Face

Just as Moses knew God directly and communicated with him personally throughout his ministry, so Jesus could say "I know him, I come from him, and he sent me" (John 7:29). On many other occasions he made it clear that he had seen God face-to-face, such as in these words "Not that anyone has ever seen the Father except him who is from God – he has seen the Father" (John 6:46). The most telling comparison at this point is found in two passages which speak of the effect of the close relationship Moses and Jesus had with God. The first tells what happened when Moses spoke with God face-to-face:

Moses did not know that the skin of his face shone while he talked with him. Exodus 34:29-30

When the image of the invisible God was directly revealed through Jesus as God spoke of him as his own Beloved Son, we read:

And he was transfigured before them, and his face shone like the sun, and his garments became white as light. Matthew 17:2

No other prophet could claim such a distinction. No one else knew God face-to-face in such a way that his face shone as he communed with him. Certainly there are no evidences anywhere in the Koran or any other Muslim records that Muhammad ever emulated the experience. Even the story of Al-Mir'aj, his supposed ascension to heaven, do not state that his face ever shone in any way.

3. Jesus Likewise Performed Great Miracles

There are numerous stories of great miracles that Jesus did during his life, but once again a direct parallel with Moses will help to emphasize the likeness between them. Both of them had power to control the sea, a feat never emulated by any other prophet.

Moses stretched out his hand over the sea; and the Lord caused the sea to go back by a strong east wind. Exodus 14:21

Other prophets after Moses had power over rivers (Joshua 3:13, 2 Kings 2:14), but no one could emulate Moses' great miracle of controlling the sea until Jesus stood over the Sea of Galilee one night, and during a raging storm, calmed it with just three words "Peace – be still" (Mark 4:39). His disciples exclaimed:

What manner of man is this, that even the winds and the sea obey him? Matthew 8:27

One of Moses' greatest miracles was to feed the people of Israel in the wilderness of Sinai with bread known as manna which appeared on the ground every day. When the Jews saw Jesus feed five thousand people besides women and children from only five loaves of bread and two fishes so that there was enough left over to fill twelve baskets, they immediately recalled Moses' prophecy.

When the people saw the sign which he had done, they said, "This is indeed the prophet who is to come into the world." John 6:14

When they saw the sign, they declared that Jesus was the prophet, the one foretold by Moses in Deuteronomy 18:18. There can be no doubt from all these evidences that Jesus is the prophet whose coming was prophesied by Moses and not Muhammad. The evidences relating to the unique features of his life, specifically named in Deuteronomy 34:10-11 as the ones which would identify the coming prophet, prove conclusively that he was the one of whom God spoke to the people of Israel.

The Brethren

Muslim: The promise was of a prophet to come from among the brethren of the Israelites. Abraham had two sons, Ishmael and Isaac, and their brethren were the Ishmaelites. Muhammad was descended from Ishmael and he is therefore the prophet.

This is one of the favorite arguments of Muslims in trying to prove that the prophet foretold in Deuteronomy 18:18 was Muhammad. They emphasize the words "from among their brethren," assuming that it is the "brethren" of the Israelites as a nation that are spoken of in the prophecy. A brief survey of the context of the passage shows quite conclusively that it was not the Ishmaelites who were in mind.

The Brethren of the Levites

The prophecy in Deuteronomy 18:18 is set in a context of a whole discourse where God gave Moses certain directions about the future conduct of the people of Israel once they reached the promised land, especially the Levites, the priestly tribe. A look at the first two verses of the chapter will reveal very clearly who God was speaking of when he said he would raise up for them a prophet from among their brethren.

The Levitical priests, that is, all the tribes of Levi, shall have no portion or inheritance with Israel . . . They shall have no inheritance among their brethren.
Deuteronomy 18:1-2

It is abundantly clear here that they mean the Levites, and that their brethren means the other tribes of Israel. No honest method of interpretation can possibly yield any other conclusion. Therefore, the correct interpretation of Deuteronomy 18:18 must be: "I will raise up for them (the Levites) a prophet like you from among their brethren (the other eleven tribes of Israel)."
Therefore the passage cannot refer to the Ishmaelites and the prophecy most certainly cannot apply to Muhammad, the Prophet of Islam.

It is interesting to note that, throughout the Old Testament, the expression "their brethren" often occurs, and in every case it refers to one of the tribes of Israel as distinct from the one actually mentioned. A typical example is found in the following verse where there can be no doubt as to who the brethren are:

But the children of Benjamin would not listen to the voice of their brethren, the children of Israel. Judges 20:13

Here "their brethren" is specifically stated to be the other member of the nation of Israel as distinct from the tribe of Benjamin. In the same way Deuteronomy 18:18 refers to the other tribes of Israel as distinct from the tribe of Levi. In another passage we read that Moses said to the people of Israel:

One from among your brethren you shall set a king over you; you may not put a foreigner over you, who is not your brother. Deuteronomy 17:5

Only one of the brethren of the Israelites could be appointed as king over the nation. They were not allowed to place a foreigner, such as an Ishmaelite, over them. Here the principle is reinforced that the prophet who was to come from among "their brethren" was to be an Israelite, only not one of the people of the tribe of Levi. In Europe for many centuries it has been customary for monarchs to come from various nations so as to maintain a close relationship between the various countries. German, British, French and Greek princess have often intermarried with princesses or other royal women from other nations. In Israel, however, there was an express command to the people that they were not to put anyone from another nation over them as king, because they had been set apart as the people of God, distinct from the pagan nations around them.

Jesus the Prophet from Among Their Brethren

Do we have any evidences, however, to prove that Jesus qualifies as the prophet foretold in this particular context? The New Testament quite clearly records that Jesus was descended from Judah through the line of David. He is expressly said to have descended from "Judah, the son of Jacob" (Luke 3:33) and in another place we read "Now it is evident that our Lord was descended from Judah" (Hebrews 7:14). Jesus is therefore obviously the one who was to come from one of the other tribes of Israel. Together with the other evidences we have considered there can be no doubt that he is the prophet foretold in Deuteronomy 18:18. Muhammad meets none of the vital criterion for qualifying for this office.

Other Muslim argument in favor of Muhammad also does not stand the test of close scrutiny. God said of the prophet to come "I will put my words in his mouth" and Muslims say that, by revealing the Koran to Muhammad who repeated it to his followers, the prophecy was fulfilled. According to Islam, however, the Tawraat was equally so revealed to Moses, the Zabur to David, and the Injil to Jesus. So each of them had the words of God in their mouths. To Jeremiah God said "Behold I have put my words in your mouth" (Jeremiah 1:9).

Likewise God went on to say to Moses "he shall speak to them all that I command him." Jesus once said to his disciples:

For I have not spoken on my own authority; the Father who sent me has himself given me commandment what to say and what to speak John 12:49

The Muslims can raise no unique evidence to prove, from the context of the prophecy, that Muhammad was the prophet foretold in Deuteronomy 18:8.

Another argument centers on the questions the Jews once put to John the Baptist after he denied that he was the Christ, namely whether he was Elijah and, if not, whether he was the Prophet? (John 1:21) They argue that the Jews distinguished between Elijah, the Christ and the Prophet, and that they were, in order, John the Baptist, Jesus and Muhammad.

Nothing conclusive can be drawn from the speculations of the Jews, however. Once they said of Jesus "This is indeed the prophet" (John 7:40). On another occasion they concluded he was "one of the prophets" (Matthew 16:14), on another "a prophet" (Mark 6:15) and thought of him as both Elijah (Mark 6:15) and as possibly John the Baptist himself (Matthew 16:14). Nothing conclusive can be drawn from their guesswork.

There can be no doubt, from all we have considered, that it was Jesus Christ and not Muhammad whose coming was foretold by Moses in Deuteronomy 18:18.

Jesus's Promise of the Coming Comforter

Muslim: According to your Bible did not Jesus speak of another prophet to come after him whom he called the Comforter? This was obviously a prophecy of the coming of our holy prophet Muhammad. The Koran even confirms the prophecy.

The greatest of all the Muslim claims that Muhammad is foretold in the Bible comes from the promise of Jesus to his disciples, recorded four times in John's Gospel, that he would be followed by yet another person sent from God whom he called the Comforter, one who would guide them into all truth. From the earliest centuries of

Islam Muslim scholars have endeavored to prove that the Comforter was Muhammad, the Prophet of Islam. Of all the challenges made to Christians in witness among Muslims, this one is undoubtedly the most frequent. Yet even here Christians have, when responding to their arguments, tremendous opportunities for witness to Muslims of who the comforter really is – the Holy Spirit – and how he fulfills the redeeming work of Jesus.

Muslim Arguments about the Comforter
It is in the following texts that Muslims believe they have proof that Muhammad was duly foretold by Jesus, in terms of the Koranic text, which states that they would find his coming prophesied in the Injil as well as the Tawraat (Sura 4:157):

But the Comforter, the Holy Spirit, whom the father will send in my name, he will teach you all things, and bring to your remembrance all that I have said to you. John 14:26

Nevertheless, I tell you the truth: it is to your

advantage that I go away, for if I do not go away, the Comforter will not come to you; but if I go, I will send him to you. John 16:7

Both these sayings come from a lengthy discourse of Jesus on the last night he was with his disciples before his crucifixion. On two other occasions in the same discourse he again spoke of the coming Comforter (John 14:16, 15:26). Muslims claim that he was undoubtedly speaking of Muhammad for the following reasons:

1. Muhammad Led the World into all the Truth

Muslims argue that, when Jesus said the Comforter will "teach you all things," this was fulfilled in their Prophet who in delivering the Koran, taught the world all it needs to know about God, his laws, and the way of life he expects his servants to follow. So likewise, when Jesus said "he will declare
to you the things that are to come" (John 16:13), Muhammad is claimed to have done exactly this as the Koran discourses at length on the Last Day (Yawma'l Akhir), The Resurrection, the Final Judgment, and the destiny of the human race to heaven (Jannat) or hell (Jahannam).

2. The Use of the Masculine Gender

Muslims often make much of the fact that, in speaking of the coming Comforter, Jesus used the masculine gender no less than eight times. They argue that, when Jesus said "He will glorify me, he will not speak on his own authority, he will guide you into all truth," etc., he was obviously speaking of a man, a prophet, and not the Holy Spirit. A spirit it is claimed, being neither male nor female, cannot be spoken of in anything but the neutral gender but, as Jesus consistently used the word he to describe the Comforter, this must refer to a male prophet, namely Muhammad.

3. The Comforter Was to Come after Jesus
The third argument commonly used by Muslims to prove their case is that, as Jesus said the Comforter would not come until he had gone away, this must mean Muhammad. Once again, they reason, it cannot refer to the Holy Spirit because, according to the Bible, the Holy Spirit had always been there. David prayed that God would not take his Spirit from him (Psalm 51:11) while John the Baptist was said to have been filled with Holy Spirit from his mother's womb (Luke 1:15).

The Christian Response to these Arguments

There are simple answers to these three arguments. A careful study of the whole context of the relevant verses shows quite clearly that Jesus was speaking of the Holy Spirit who indeed came down within ten days after Jesus' ascension as he had promised (Acts 2:1-21).

Firstly, the Holy Spirit duly brought to the remembrance of Jesus' disciples all that he had said to them. John only wrote his Gospel some sixty years after Jesus' crucifixion and resurrection, yet he was able to record the whole of his last discourse to his disciples accurately in no less than four chapters (John 13:1 - 16:33). The complete teaching which followed is recorded, not in the Koran, but in the twenty-seven books of the New Testament. All its teaching is inspired by God through the Holy Spirit (2 Timothy 3:16) and none of it is subject to man's interpretation, because it never came through human impulse since "men, moved by the Holy Spirit, spoke from God" (2 Peter 1:21).

Secondly, throughout the Bible both God and the Holy Spirit are always referred to in the masculine gender. "He is your Praise, he is your God" (Deuteronomy 10:21) is a typical example of its constant use to describe the Divine being even though God is not man, but spirit (John 4:24). The Muslim argument can be turned on its head by referring to a passage of the Koran where Allah is spoken of in the masculine gender no less than seven times in quick succession (Sura 59:22-24). "He is Allah and there is no god besides who he is" is the middle text (v. 23) and it begins and ends with the masculine huwa ("he is") and not the neutral hiya ("it is"). If Allah, who is spirit and not man, can nonetheless be spoken of in the masculine gender in the Koran, why can the Holy Spirit likewise not be spoken of prophet, rather he is expressly identified as the Holy Spirit (John 14:26).

Thirdly, Jesus not only said he had to go away before the Comforter would come, but also promised that he would personally send him to his own disciples, to Peter, James, John and the rest. "I will send him to you" he said (John 16:7), not to Arabs in Mecca or Medina six centuries later. It could hardly have been to the disciples' advantage if the Comforter was not to come almost immediately after Jesus left the earth. When he was about to ascend to heaven Jesus expressly told them to wait a short while in Jerusalem until they received the Holy Spirit before they went out proclaiming the Gospel

(Acts 1:4-5). The Comforter had indeed been present in the world before this time, but now he was to be poured out in a new way right into the hearts of all who believed in Jesus. They had experienced the ministry and presence of Jesus with them for three years, but now his presence was to be known in a way even more to their advantage – by the fact of the Spirit actually living within them.

"His Name Shall be Ahmad" in the Koran

Muslim: According to the Koran Jesus specifically predicted the coming of Muhammad as the "Praised One." This was his actual prophecy. You Christians have since changed the original word Periklutos ("Praised") into Paracletos ("Comforter").

Muslims particularly concentrate on Jesus' promise of a coming Comforter because it seems to confirm a similar text in the Koran where he is said to have expressly predicted the coming of Muhammad:

And remember Jesus, son of Mary, said "O Children of Israel! I am a messenger of Allah to you, confirming what is before me from the Tawraat, and announcing tidings of a

messenger to follow me whose name shall
be Ahmad." Sura 61:6

Although the prediction is not of
Muhammad by his actual name, Muslim
scholars point out that Ahmad comes from
the same three root letters as his own name,
hmd, meaning "praise." It seems
Muhammad knew that Jesus had spoken of
someone to follow him, but had not done so
by name and, for this reason, he avoided any
mention of himself personally in adapting
the prophecy to the Koran using a title as
close to his name as he could to ensure the
necessary inference that it was him.

Periklutos or Parakletos?

The original word in John's Gospel
translated as "Comforter" is paracletos,
meaning (as the English equivalent
"paraclete" implies) one who clings closely
as a counselor or mentor. It never means
"one who is praised." It is obvious from the
sayings of Jesus that the original word is the
correct one as everything he had to say
about the Comforter related precisely to this
concept of a close adviser.

"He will take what is mine and declare it to
you" is typical of the description Jesus gave

to the Holy Spirit. He was to dwell in hearts of his disciples and would give them an insight and guidance into God's ways and the power to fulfill them from within their own souls. He would come to convict the world of sin, righteousness and judgement as God's agent speaking through the witness and proclamations of Jesus' disciples.

Nevertheless Muslims have, in their writings, argued that the Christian world has corrupted the original saying of Jesus and that it incorporated the word periklutos which means "Praised One." This roughly coincides with the title Ahmad in the Koran, having the same basic meaning. Is there any substance in the Muslim claim? Are there any evidences to prove it?

1. Periklutos is not a Biblical Word
There is no manuscript evidence whatsoever that the original word may have been periklutos. In fact the word nowhere appears in the Greek New Testament and is accordingly not a Biblical Word. The Muslim claim is based, not on any kind of concrete, factual

testimony, but purely on a supposition to suit themselves.

2. The Word does not Fit into the Context

As pointed out already, the definition of the coming one whom Jesus promised was primarily of a counselor and advocate. There is nothing in all four sayings of Jesus about the Comforter to support the contention that he was to be "the Praised One." On the contrary, when Jesus said "he will not speak on his own authority, but whatever he hears he will speak" (John 16:13) he made it clear he would specifically not drawn attention to himself. "He will glorify me" Jesus went on to say (John 16:14), meaning he would give praise to Jesus through the witness of his followers rather than claim any praise for himself.

3. It is Muslims who are Changing the Bible

The irony of this issue is that we have here clear evidence of a Muslim attempt to do what they have always wrongly accused the Christian world of doing, namely of trying to change the Bible to suit their own preferences! They have had to resort to a strange distortion to make the prophecy of Jesus fit Muhammad, and purely to bring into being some kind of connection with the name (or title) Ahmad in the Koran. It is clear they cannot prove their point directly from the Biblical texts as they stand.

There is no justification for the claim that the original word used by Jesus was periklutos or any Hebrew equivalent of it. Most importantly, as we have seen, it does not linguistically fit the context of his sayings.

The Title Ahmad in the Koran

There have been a number of disputes over the years about the employment of the word Ahmad in the Koran. Today it is a common first name among Muslims throughout the world, but there is no evidence in Arabian records dating back to the time of Muhammad that it was ever used as a personal name in the early centuries of Islam. It almost certainly came into popular use as a result of this text of the Koran.

It is more probable that the actual form of the word in Sura 61:1, ahmadu, was a simple adjective in the Arabic language of this time. This is supported by the fact that, in the sayings of Jesus we have considered, a proper name of the coming comforter is entirely omitted.

It is also very interesting to note that in one of the early codices of the Koran which Uthman ordered to be burnt, namely that of the expert reciter Ubayy ibn Ka'b, Sura 61:6 reads somewhat differently. He omitted the conclusion "his name will be Ahmad" (ismuhu ahmad) and in its place records Jesus as saying that he was announcing a prophet who would bear the seal of Allah from his prophets and messengers (khatumullaahu bihil-anbiyaa' wal-rusuli).

From a Christian perspective Sura 61:1 is an attempt to modify the prophecy of Jesus about the coming of the Holy Spirit to apply it instead to the Prophet of Islam. Some centuries before his time a counterfeit messiah named Mani also tried to apply the prophecy to himself and it seems that it was well known in the vicinity of Arabia during the centuries following the time of Jesus. It would only be natural for someone like Muhammad, believing he was the last of the messengers of Allah, to want to secure it in some deliberate way for himself – hence the adaptation of the title into the name Ahmad in the Koran.

The Holy Spirit: The Promised Comforter

Muslim: You cannot deny that Jesus did speak specifically of another messenger of God to follow him. As he was only one of a long line of prophets and apostles sent by God, is it not surely logical to assume that the Comforter was to be Muhammad?

In discussion with Muslims on this subject it is useful to take just one of the four sayings of Jesus about the coming Comforter, and to show from it that he could only have been speaking of the Holy Spirit. At the same time a healthy witness can be given to just how the Holy Spirit brings true believers into a relationship of personal unity with God himself. The ideal text for this purpose is this one:

And I will pray the Father, and he will give you another Comforter, to be with you forever, even the Spirit of Truth, whom the world cannot receive, because it neither sees him nor knows him; you know him, for he dwells with you, and will be in you. John 14:16-17

There are a number of reasons why this passage can only apply to the Holy Spirit and not to the Prophet of Islam, Muhammad.

Another Comforter: The Spirit of Truth

By applying sound principles of interpretation to this passage we will find at least seven reasons for concluding that the promised Comforter was the divine Holy Spirit who Jesus promised would come to his disciples shortly after his ascension to heaven.

1. He will give you Another Comforter

Jesus specifically told his disciples that he would send the promised Comforter to them. He repeated the promise later by saying "I will send him to you" (John 16:7). Thus the coming of the Spirit of Truth, also specifically declared to be the Holy Spirit (John 14:26), was something the disciples of Jesus were to expect in their time and environment. Muhammad only appeared six centuries later.

2. He will give you Another Comforter

If, as Muslims claim, the original title was periklutos, then the sentence would have read "He will give you another praised one." It not only makes no sense, but is completely out of context. What Jesus is saying here is simply: "I have been your comforter, your counselor and adviser. I have yet many things to teach you, but I will send you another counselor and guide like me." He had come from God as a spirit from heaven and had taken human form for the duration of his short life on earth. He would send another spirit from above to fulfill his ministry to his followers.

The Koran interestingly confirms that Jesus came from God, calling him a "spirit from him" (ruhun-minhu), a title given to no other human being in the book (Sura 58:22). In the only other instance where the Koran speaks of a ruhun-minhu, it speaks of a spirit whom God sends into the hearts of true believers to strengthen them – precisely who the Holy Spirit is. So the Koran agrees that there were only two spirits whom God has ever sent from himself into the world, Jesus Christ and the Holy Spirit, each one a paracletos, a guide and mentor, to comfort and lead the true followers of God on earth.

3. To be With You Forever

When Muhammad came to the fore as the Prophet of Islam in Arabia in the 7th century after Christ, he did not stay with his companions forever, but died at the age of 62 years. He was buried in Medina where his body has lain for nearly fourteen centuries. Jesus stated that the promised Comforter, however, would be with his disciples forever and the Holy Spirit has done just that, living in the hearts of all true followers of Jesus to this day.

4. The Spirit of Truth whom the World Cannot Receive

The Koran says that Muhammad came as a universal messenger to all mankind (Sura 34:28). Muslims believe that one day the whole world will submit to Islam and become followers of their Prophet. If so Jesus could not have been speaking about him for he declared that the world as a whole cannot receive the Spirit of Truth. Only the true followers of Jesus, who turn to him as their Savior and Lord, can be born anew of the Holy Spirit and become heirs of eternal life.

5. You Know Him

It is quite obvious from this statement that Jesus' disciples already knew the Spirit of Truth. As Muhammad was only born more than five hundred years later it could not have been him. The Comforter was a Spirit with whom the disciples were already

familiar. The next clause states precisely
how he was already known to them.

6. He dwells With You

When Jesus first came to John the Baptist to
be baptized by him at the very beginning of
his ministry, the heavens were opened and
John himself records what happened next:

I saw the Spirit descend as a dove from
heaven, and it remained on him. I myself
did not know him; but he who sent me to
baptize with water said to me, 'He on whom
you see the Spirit descend and remain, this
is he who baptizes with the Holy Spirit'.
John 1:32-33

The Spirit of Truth was at all times in the
person of Jesus himself, and in this manner
the disciples of Jesus had already come to
know him. At no time could Muhammad
have been said to have already been with
Jesus' disciples.

7. He Will be In You

As the Spirit was already in Jesus, so it
would also enter into and be forever present
in the hearts of Jesus' disciples once he had
returned to heaven. This happened on the
day of Pentecost when the Holy Spirit was

poured out on all who heard the Word of God and the Gospel of Jesus for the first time. God's love continues to be poured into the hearts of those who turn in faith to Jesus through the same Holy Spirit given to them (Romans 5:5). The Greek word here is en, meaning "right inside you." The promise clearly cannot refer to Muhammad who has never entered personally into the hearts of all true Christian believers.

Christians cannot only easily refute Muslim arguments in favor of Muhammad as the promised Comforter, but as you can surely see, have at this point an excellent base to witness effectively to Muslims.

APPENDIX E

The Love of God in the Koran and the Bible

THE LOVE OF GOD IN THE Koran AND THE Bible
1. The Great and First Commandment
2. The Love of God in the Koran
3. The Fatherhood of God in the Bible
4. The Revelation of God's Love in Jesus Christ
5. Knowing God's Love through the Holy Spirit

The Love of God in the Koran and the Bible

"You shall keep the commandments of the Lord your God, by walking in his ways and by fearing him." Deuteronomy 8:6

Moses spoke these words to the Children of Israel shortly before he died. No one need marvel at them for our Creator naturally has the right to demand that his creatures obey his laws and commandments. It is our bounden duty to keep God's laws and we deservedly incur his wrath if we do not do so. Just as a servant is obliged to render loyal service to his master, so it is the duty

of all men to fear God and keep his
commandments (Ecclesiastes 12:13). If we
were to ask, however, which is the greatest
of all God's commandments, what would
the answer be? Would it be simply that we
must believe in the oneness of God and
perform the duties he lays upon us? Or is
some higher obligation expected of us? Let
us hear Moses again to discover whether
indeed there is a greater duty upon us toward
God other than that of simply keeping his
laws.

"What does the Lord your God require of
you, but to fear the Lord Your God, to walk
in all his ways, to love him, to serve the
Lord your God with all your heart and with
all your soul." Deuteronomy 10:12

Once again the command to serve God is
given to us, but now a new dimension has
come into the command. It is found in these
three words: "to love him." Principally the
difference made by these three words is that
our service to God is not to be merely the
servile exercise of the duties he lays upon
us, but clearly must be the expression of the
affections of our own hearts toward him.
Moses very carefully made his people
known that such is the service God expects
from men. The mere discharge of duty is

not what he requires. The only service he will accept from men is that which flows from love that proceeds from the heart. Moses emphasizes this fact again and again during his last words to the Children of Israel:

"You shall therefore LOVE the Lord your God." Deuteronomy 11:1
"I command you this day, to love the Lord your God." Deuteronomy 11:13

In his eyes, therefore, it is of supreme importance that we serve God out of love and that all that we do should be done in love toward him.

1. The Great and First Commandment

Centuries later a Jewish scribe came up to Jesus and put a question to him to test his interpretation of the law to see whether he agreed with the opinions of the Jewish elders:

"Teacher, which is the great commandment in the law?" Matthew 22:36

The Jews had studied God's laws exhaustively and this one wished to test

Jesus to see what answer he would give him to this question. At once Jesus said:

"You shall love the Lord your God with all your heart, and with all your soul, and with all your mind. This is the great and first commandment." Matthew 22:37-38

The command to love God is therefore the greatest and foremost of all his commandments. All other laws and all the teachings of the prophets are summed up in this one law to love the Lord with all our hearts, souls and minds. No other law can faithfully be kept unless it is kept in a spirit of love.

What, however, is love? Can we say that by our efforts to obey God's laws we automatically show that we love him? That obedience to his commands is an essential aspect of love toward him is not to be disputed. No one who disobeys his commands loves him. Nevertheless, the mere performance of religious duties is not proof of the presence of love. Men who endeavor to serve God may do so through fear, pride or prospect of reward. Love, therefore, is not necessarily the motivation behind such service. We must serve and obey God if we love him, but this service must be done out of love, and must be motivated by love. One of the closest disciples of Jesus, the Apostle John, put it as follows:

"And this is love, that we follow his commandments; this is the commandment, as you have heard from the beginning, that you follow love." 2 John 6

There is clearly something intensely deep about obedience that grows out of love. When we analyze the basic principles of love, we find certain essential features which must be present for this love to be truly exercised.

Firstly, love must be genuine (Romans 12:9). It must be an uninhibited expression of the affections of the heart. There must be complete freedom for such love to be genuinely exercised. If there is any presence of fear in the heart, love cannot be openly displayed. The fear of punishment will automatically disqualify the one who has it from genuinely loving the one he fears. All his service toward that person will be done with the purpose of alleviating the wrath of that person toward him. Such service, therefore, springs not from love but from self-motivation. The man who serves God because he has no assurance of forgiveness from God, and seeks by this service to obtain that forgiveness, has his own welfare at heart. He most certainly does. He does not truly love God for love is selfless. Love, as a motivation of the heart, knows no partners. For love to be genuine there cannot be any other factor affecting the service of the one who seeks to express that love.

"There is no fear in love, but perfect love casts out fear. For fear has to do with punishment, and he who fears is not perfected in love." 1 John 4:18

Accordingly, if a man would serve God and keep his commandments through genuine love, there may not be any fear of God's wrath in his heart. This makes it essential, from the outset, for there to be complete knowledge of forgiveness in the heart of the man who would to serve God out of love. That forgiveness must be experienced now, and may not be an uncertain prospect at a time to come in the future.

If a man is unsure of God's complete remission of his sins, and if he does not enjoy a state of permanent forgiveness for all that he may think or do, he cannot possibly serve God out of genuine love.

Though he professes love toward God, he must really serve him with the primary objective of obtaining his forgiveness and alleviating his wrath. Such service is, as we have seen, principally self-motivated for it seeks approval for itself rather than the glory of God. Therefore, if we are to truly love God, we must first experience the perfect knowledge of his forgiveness in our hearts. For our love to be genuine, a condition of complete peace with God must reign within us.

Secondly, love must be impressive. Unless deeds of love flow from the heart, there is no love in the heart of the worshiper. Love is an empty vacuum unless it manifests itself in appropriate ways.
"Little children, let us not love in word or speech but in deed and truth." 1 John 3:18

From the side of man the obvious form of this expression is through heartfelt obedience to God's commands. As Jesus himself put it on the last night he was with his disciples:

"He who has my commandments and keeps them, he it is who loves me." John 14:21

God will discover no love in us toward him if we do not obey his commandments. Nevertheless, if it is God's desire not only that we should obey his laws but that we should do so completely out of love, then it is essential that there be in the nature of God that which merits this love. The expression of man's love toward God must be in response to, and in gratitude for, the manifestation of God's love toward man. If men have knowledge of the love of God through some definite revelation of it in the history of God's dealings with them, then it is not only possible but essential that men express their appreciation of this fact through love toward God.

In one of the most beautiful books in the Bible, the Song of Solomon, we have a splendid example of this principle. The book concerns the deepest affections of a man and his bride for one another. On one occasion when he was apart from her, she sought him desperately, saying to her companions:

"I adjure you, O daughters of Jerusalem, if you find my beloved, that you tell him I am sick with love." Song of Solomon 5:8

Mildly surprised by this determined quest for the presence of the one she loved (which they apparently did not share for their own partners), her companions said to her in reply:

"What is your beloved more than another beloved?" Song of Solomon 5:9

In a lengthy reply she detailed the worth of her loved one and showed that she considered him to excel in every respect, from his head to his feet. He was, in her view, distinguished among ten thousand. It was little wonder that a deeper expression of love for her beloved sprang from her heart than from those of her companions for their spouses. She summed up his worth in these words:

"His speech is most sweet, and he is altogether desirable. This is my beloved and this is my friend, O daughters of Jerusalem." Song of Solomon 5:16

Because he excelled in honor all the other men of her nation, she naturally expressed a deeper affection for him than her companions did for their husbands. With these principles in mind it must surely be true that those who see the very best of

God's love toward men will respond in the most fervent way in love toward him. Those who see God's love in the works of nature and the many providential graces he extends toward us will find it possible to express love to him in return. But if God should choose to demonstrate his love for mankind by giving of his very own self to redeem them from sin, no men on earth will know the capacity of love toward God which those have who are in fact partakers of this redemption. The deeper the revelation of God's love toward mankind, the deeper will be the response of love toward him in those who believe in and appropriate the effects of this love.

Thirdly, love must be mutual. No man will be able to sustain love in his heart toward a woman who scorns that love and within a marriage love can only really develop where the spouses reciprocate their love for each other. If we are to be rooted and grounded in love for one another, it is necessary that such love be mutual for a perfect balance to take effect. An achievement of such mutual love will result in such an expression as this from the one who shares in that love:

"I am my beloved's and my beloved is mine." Song of Solomon 6:3

Love is the greatest of all abiding graces (1 Corinthians 13:13). When God commands men to love him with all their hearts, he is drawing on the greatest of all virtues in doing so. He seeks the best form of worship he could possibly obtain from them. But for such worship to develop to its highest possible potential in men, the expression of love between men and God must be mutual. Not only is it necessary for God to manifest his love toward men but he must also allow men the fullest possible experience of that love in their own hearts for such mutual love to truly be present.

Therefore, let us at this stage formulate our conclusions about the "great commandment" that each of us should love God with all his heart, soul and mind. This commandment demonstrates the will of God that men should give of their very best for him. Nothing less than genuine love, expressed in positive ways, is acceptable to God. But for this to be possible on the part of men, three initiatives are needed on the part of God. They are these:

1. He must offer forgiveness of sins to all from whom he expects this love so that it may be real and undisturbed by fear.

171

2.   He must manifest and reveal his love for men in such a way that they can respond to him in love.

3. He must allow men the personal knowledge of his love and a living experience of it in their hearts if a mutual, abiding communion based on love is to develop between him and them.

It may seem strange, even presumptuous, to some men to say that God "must" do these things, but when all the implications are considered it is surely obvious that for creatures to obey the commandment to love God, these factors must of necessity be present. Otherwise men cannot possibly exert such genuine love toward God as he expects of them.

2. The Love of God in the Koran

Christianity and Islam have different views of God. Both the Bible and the Koran claim to be the Word of God, but the theology of God is often strikingly different in these two books. What we are particularly concerned about here, however, is to discover in which book we find the best revelation of God's love toward men. Let us begin by studying briefly the teaching of the Koran about the love of God.

Firstly, there is in the Koran an exhortation to men to love God. Perhaps the best verse in the Koran which contains this injunction is this one:
"Say, If ye love Allah, follow me; Allah will love you and forgive you your sins." Sura 3:31

Significantly, however, one does not find in this verse (nor in any other in the Koran) the command to love God with "all your heart, soul and mind." The reason is fairly clear from the verse itself. The hearer is exhorted to love God so that he may thereby obtain God's love and forgiveness. The basic object, therefore, of this love is the acquittal and approval of God for the believer. Accordingly the motivation for such love must be the welfare and comfort of the believer. It is not suggested in the Koran that such love must be exercised in a disinterested and selfless manner with the glory of God foremost in the believer's mind. On the contrary the object of such love is really the believer himself. He seeks by this love fundamentally to turn aside God's wrath and to gain his approval in its place. Now this is not the fruit of genuine love. Such love, as we have seen, must be the exercise of the purest affections of the heart toward God – it cannot be accompanied by an ancillary motive such as the principal objective of obtaining God's forgiveness.

For this reason it is therefore quite significant that the Koran does not exhort the believer to love God with all his heart. Such love from the heart is essentially selfless in nature. That which seeks its own security does not proceed from the heart. It is not the expression of the deepest affections of the very kernel of a man's being. Love in the latter sense seeks principally the glory of its object – but that which strives for the approval of God and considers primarily its own prospects of forgiveness is fundamentally self-motivated. It cannot be described as genuine love and certainly he who loves God chiefly to obtain his forgiveness is not fulfilling the royal commandment – indeed what Jesus called the "great and first commandment" to love God with all his heart, soul and mind. As we saw earlier, the fear of God's wrath disqualifies the potential for genuine love in the heart.

The Koran does not give the believer any total assurance of the forgiveness of all his sins this side of the grave. Accordingly it is hardly surprising that it sets the prospect of forgiveness at the end of life as the reward of service to God. Even then there is no complete assurance that the believer will be forgiven and the believer can only die in the hope of God's mercy (Sura 17:57). It must again be stressed, however, that such service is done purely out of love toward oneself with the welfare of the self at heart. Only when the believer begins with the total knowledge of God's forgiveness can he serve God freely out of genuine love. As long as he fears God's wrath, he cannot possibly exercise real love toward God with the glory of God as the principal concern of his heart.

Accordingly it must be concluded that the teaching of the Koran does not meet the needs of genuine love. It leaves presently undecided the fact of forgiveness and its exhortations to men to love God are given with one chief objective – the realization of his acquittal and approval. In such circumstances a man cannot honestly love God with all his heart. He cannot express such love without some prospect of acquittal and acceptance with God foremost in his soul and mind.

Secondly, we find that the Koran says very little about the expression of God's love for mankind. Almost invariably the Koran speaks of this love as an expression of approval of those who do good. This verse gives a typical example of this fact (and has the same theme as the others on this subject):

"Spend your wealth for the cause of Allah, and be not cast by your own hands to ruin; and do good. Lo! Allah loveth the beneficent." Sura 2:135

Throughout the Koran we read that Allah loves those who do good and does not love those who do evil. This means principally that he approves of those who do good and accordingly disapproves of those who do evil. In every case where the expression occurs in the Koran it can easily be translated "approves of" instead of "loves" without any change in the meaning of the expression at all. The knowledge and realization of this approval will also only be known at the Last Day. This is virtually all that the Koran says about the love of God toward mankind.

In our view this is insufficient to awaken in men heartfelt love toward God. There is no present expression of that love from God which can evoke the response of love in men toward him. Indeed the Koran often appeals to that which is visible in nature as a proof of God's existence and character. But it is the order in nature itself which reveals the existence and sovereignty of the one true God (Romans 1:20). The Koran does not reveal this fact – it is merely appealing to the revelation of it in nature. But apart from this the Koran tells us really nothing about the depth of the love of God toward men outside of that which can be discovered in nature. It does not disclose any great act of love in the history of God's dealings with men which should cause the response of heartfelt love toward him in return. To put it in a nutshell, there is no definite expression of love in the heart of God toward men in the Koran. No proof of deep affection toward mankind is given at all.

The filial love that a father has for his own children and the revelation of that love is not found in the relationship between God and men in the Koran. It has no concept of the Fatherhood of God, and whereas God is most commonly called "the Father" in the Bible, no such exalted title is found in the Koran. Furthermore, there is no manifestation of God's love toward mankind, which is of the greatest form of love – that of self-denial and self-sacrifice. One does not find in the Koran a unilateral display of love in God, which expresses itself on behalf of mankind in such a way that God is willing to give of himself to prove and manifest that love. Indeed, even in respect of the teaching that he "loves" those who do good we do not find that this love is an expression of sentiment in the heart of God toward the faithful. In the context of this Hadith – which is very consistent with the teaching of the Koran about the attitude of Allah toward mankind (Sura 5:18) – we see very clearly the total lack of sentiment in this love:

"Verily Allah created Adam and then rubbed his back with His right hand and took out a progeny from him and said: I created these for Paradise and with the actions of the inmates of Paradise which they will do. Afterwards, he rubbed his back with His hand and took out a progeny from him and said: I created these for Hell and with the actions of the inmates of Hell which they will do." (Mishkat Al-Masabih, Vol.3, p.107)

We are constrained to conclude that there is no expression of glorious, heartfelt love of

God in the Koran which would enable men in return to honor his desire, and command that we should love him with all our 'hearts, souls and minds.' If God in his very own nature does not have heartfelt love toward men, they cannot possibly be expected to express such love toward him in return.

Lastly we find, as a matter of course after what has already been said, that there is, in the teaching of the Koran, no capacity for mutual love between God and men, such as that between a man and his wife, which we discover in the Song of Solomon. It is not possible, according to the Koran, for men to actually experience God's love in their very own hearts, such as a son's experience of his father's love, and a wife of her husband's love. God is indeed called the "Loving One" (Al - Wadud) in the Koran, but only on two occasions (Suras 11:90, 85:14). This statement, however, does not imply the depth of love in the nature of God such as is found in the Biblical declaration "God is love" (1 John 4:8). Instead one of the great theologians in Islamic history, Al-Ghazzali, is at pains to inform us that the expression "The Loving One" means far less than the title would seem to indicate. In his work on the names of God in the Koran entitled, Al-Maqsad Al-Asna, he states that this title in the Koran is a lesser one, for example, than "The Merciful" (ar-Rahim) – an opinion with which we find ourselves compelled to agree, for God is called "The Merciful" over two hundred times in the Koran, but "The Loving One" only twice. Al-Ghazzali explains this love as consisting solely of objective acts of kindness and expressions of approval. He denies that there is any subjectivity in the love of God, that is, that God feels any love in his own heart toward mankind.

"He remains above the feeling of love."
(Al-Maqsad Al-Asna, p. 91).

How anyone can be "above" the feeling of love is not at all clear. Love is the greatest of all virtues and anyone who does not feel love in the inmost part of his being must surely be below this excellent grace – indeed far below it. But if it is indeed true that God is devoid of such subjective love toward mankind, then men cannot develop love in their hearts toward him, especially to the extent where they love him with all their hearts, soul and minds. Al-Ghazzali confirms this unfortunate fact by saying of God's love:

"Love and mercy are desired in respect of their objects ONLY for the sake of their fruit and benefit, and NOT because of empathy or feeling." (Al-Maqsad Al-Asna, p. 91).

The emphases are mine. Men therefore cannot have the greatest of privileges – the actual personal knowledge of God's very own love. They can receive things from God as tokens of kindness and approval, but God himself cannot be known. There is no possibility of a mutual expression of love between God and men, which can develop and grow into a wondrous communion and fellowship between him and the believer.

In these circumstances we can understand why the Koran omits the Biblical command to love God with all our hearts, souls and minds. If men cannot now obtain total assurance of forgiveness of their sins, no such genuine love is possible from them. If love is not part of God's very own being, but is only discerned in that which he gives to men; if he has not manifested deep love toward mankind in any specific way; and if he likewise withholds from men any personal experience of his very own love, then no one can possibly love him in return from his heart. There is nothing in him that can awaken the response of such love in men.

Moses and Jesus, however, both declared that the fundamental thing that God requires of men is indeed such heartfelt love. Were these men imposing on their followers an impossible command – or did they, on the contrary, have a greater and deeper knowledge of God's real nature than we find in the Koran? Because of its limited view of God's love, the Koran wisely refrains from commanding of men the greatest possible devotion to God – that of inexhaustible love from the heart. Such love could only be expected of men if God himself is far greater than the Koran makes him out to be. He will have to be far more majestic, positively greater, distinctly superior and infinitely more loving if men are to succeed in loving him with all their hearts.

God can only make such a lofty claim on the devotion of men justly if he is prepared right now to give them forgiveness of sins, reveal through some act of love that he is positively worthy of that love, and graciously extend to men the full personal knowledge of this love. Let us turn to the Bible to see whether the God of Moses and Jesus is indeed such a God.

3. The Fatherhood of God in the Bible

One of the striking features of the Christian Bible is the title "Father" for God. He is given no name in the Christian scriptures (unlike the other major religions of the world where God is always given a name in their holy books), but is always called by this title – either as "the Father" or "our Father" or "God the Father." When one considers the intimate relationship that exists between a father and his children, it is very easy to understand why we have no name for God. A man is addressed by his name when other men speak to him, but his child always calls him "father." He does not address him by his surname, for he himself bears his father's name. A name is given to a person to identify him from other men, and a child bears his father's name because of the very close relationship between them. But, in view of this intimacy, it is not necessary that a father and his son should address one another by that common name.

Therefore, if God is pleased to become the Father of his people, this must mean that he is willing to enter into such a deep personal relationship with them that no name will be in any way needed to distinguish him from them. Not only so, but the command to love him with all our hearts, souls and minds has the best prospect of fulfilment if God, in deep love for us, is willing to become our very own Father. What child is there whom his father does not love? As John put it:

"See what love the Father has given us, that we should be called children of God; and so we are." 1 John 3:1

This does not mean that God has taken to himself offspring, but rather that he is prepared to draw so near to us in love that the intimate communion which will result from this love between him and true believers can only be compared to that which exists between a loving father and his children.

Now we know that God is Judge of all the earth, and that he will deal with the sins of men on the Day of Wrath to come when his righteous judgments will be revealed. If we only know God as Judge of all we can expect no mercy on that day for men are brought before judges to be tried and condemned for their misdeeds. But a father is very different to a judge. While he may, in love and with the purpose of correction, chastise his children, it is forgiveness that really characterizes the relationship between him and them. They will always be his children and, while a servant must work to earn his place in a home, and even then only stays outside in the servant's quarters and can be dismissed at any time, a son has absolute freedom in his father's house. He does not need to work to earn a place there, nor does he reside outside the house. He cannot be dismissed, but remains the heir to all things in his father's house. That which is the father's is his also. We all surely know the expression "one day my son, this will all be yours," symbolizing the inheritance the son has to all that the father has built up during his lifetime. The following brief conversation between Jesus and his close disciple Peter brings this fact out very clearly:

"What do you think Simon? From whom do kings of the earth take toll or tribute? From their sons or from others?" And when he said "From others," Jesus said to him "Then the sons are free." Matthew 17:25-26.

In this context we must consider the Biblical teaching that God is the Father of the true Christian. If so, it means that the kingdom of heaven is the rightful home of every true believer. Because he is a child of God, he must right now be recognized as a lawful member of the household of God (Ephesians 2:19). He does not have to earn his place there, nor will he ever be dismissed from this kingdom. Indeed he will never even dwell outside it. He has as much right to a place in God's kingdom as a son has in his father's house. If God is indeed willing to share such grace with his true children, then "what love" indeed is this that he has given us. Jesus made it plain that God indeed wills to have such an intensely deep and personal relationship with the true believer:

"Fear not, little flock, for it is your Father's good pleasure to give you the kingdom."
Luke 12:32

This heart – warming promise leads us to the issue that particularly concerns us about the genuineness of love that men must have toward God. We have seen that fear of God's wrath, and the uncertainty of his forgiveness, destroy the potential for genuine love. Now, if God is prepared to be our Father, then this problem is solved immediately. By becoming our Father he has made us his children and we are therefore set free from the fear of God's wrath because we are now already assured that heaven is, and always will be, our real home.

A father always loves his own children in a very special way and no matter how well–disposed he may be toward children generally, he will always have a deeper affection for his own children than for others. The reason is simply that he sees something of himself in his own children that he does not see in others. Even though he may have sons very different to each other in looks and temperament, he will in so many ways, as he looks at them both, be able to say, "that is me." So also, if God becomes our Father, we may know that he has a special affection for us, that in some unique way he sees something of himself in us, and for this reason will assuredly never disown us.

No wonder Jesus said "Fear not." The fear of punishment has been set aside. We no longer anticipate a judge on the throne of justice before whom we must be condemned to eternal damnation for our sins. We look to a father whose kingdom is our own home and we rejoice in our hope, as children, of sharing and inheriting his glory to be revealed at the last time. Two thousand years ago Jesus instructed his disciples, in praying to God, to call on him as "our Father" (Matthew 6:9). This indicates, not a status to be longed for in the next age, but one which is presently enjoyed by every one of his disciples. As two of Jesus' followers put it, indeed his two most eminent apostles:

"We ARE children of God, and if children, then heirs, heirs of God and fellow heirs with Christ." Romans 8:17
"We ARE God's children NOW." 1 John 3:2

In these circumstances God can be known as Father NOW, and he who is a child of God need fear no wrath in the age to come. Judges execute wrath on wrongdoers and separate them from society; masters punish wayward slaves and dismiss them from their service; but fathers love their children and will always do so. So the Christian has no fear of God's wrath but only the knowledge of his love. As Jesus said to his own disciples:

"The Father himself loves you." John 16:27

Accordingly the Christian can place all his trust in God, knowing that the deep intimate relationship he shares with him will never be broken – for God is his Father, and he is one of his children. Therefore the God of the Bible meets the first requirement of genuine love from the heart. As the father of all true believers he need not be held in dread. The Day of Judgment will, instead, be a day of glory for the true Christian. God has, in these circumstances, the right to expect those who believe in him to love him genuinely with all their hearts.

There is an implied expression of the love of God for us in his declaration that he is our Father and, as a Father can be known more intimately by his children than by anyone else, the potential for mutual love here is quite obvious. Let us press on to see more fully what God has done to express his love for us so that we may know that he is indeed our Father and how he has made it possible for that love to be mutual between him and his children.

4. The Revelation of God's Love in Jesus Christ

We saw earlier that love must be expressive and, in particular, that God must manifest his love for us in some way if we are to love him with all our hearts in return. Now the Christian Bible gives such a manifestation of God's love – indeed the greatest possible expression of it that men could ever expect from him. In the following passage this revelation of God's love is fully set out:

189

"Beloved, let us love one another; for love is of God, and he who loves is born of God and knows God. He who does not love does not know God, for God is love. In this the love of God was made manifest among us, that God sent his only Son into the world, so that we might live through him. In this is love, not that we loved God but that he loved us and sent his Son to be the expiation for our sins. Beloved, if God so loved us, we also ought to love one another. No man has ever seen God; if we love one another, God abides in us and his love is perfected in us." 1 John 4:7-11.

The striking feature of this passage is the frequent recurrence of the words "God" and "love." The writer is so persuaded of the inseparable link between the two that he sums it up in these words: God IS love (1 John 4:8). This means that right in the very heart of God's own personal interest in men rests the deepest possible affection and concern for them. The love of God in this case is clearly not to be found solely outside of himself in "fruit and benefit" as Al-Ghazzali suggests. On the contrary it is that love which exists within the very nature of God and it is the love of God himself that is revealed to men in the Gospel. One can safely say that more is said of God's love in this one short passage in the Bible, than in the whole of the Koran. What was it that persuaded the Apostle John of the intensity of God's love for mankind? To what does he appeal to prove this magnificent love of God toward men of which he speaks? What had God ever done to manifest his love in such a way that he could be spoken of as the epitome of love itself? It is simply this

"In this is love, not that we love God but that he loved us and sent his Son to be the expiation of our sins." 1 John 4:10

Herein lies the proof of the depth of God's love toward us. He has done the greatest thing he could possibly do to reveal his love for us – he gave willingly his very own Son Jesus Christ to die on a cross for our sins to redeem us to himself. No greater proof of God's love can be given to mankind than this. It is no wonder that John does not appeal to anything further to make his point. He has given the very best possible proof of God's love toward men.

How may we understand the depth of this love? Let us go back in history to the prophet Abraham who was commanded by God to give his only son in a sacrifice. If we ask why God chose to ask his son of him rather than his cattle, goods or land, the answer must be that a man's own son is very different to these other things for he proceeds from his father and is part of the father's very own being. He is accordingly dearer to his father's heart than anything else. Therefore the best way that God could test Abraham's love for him was to command that he sacrifice his son for him. For surely, if Abraham would give his son for God, he would give him all things. This is precisely what mankind can, discover about God's love for the human race in the gift of his Son Jesus Christ as a sacrifice for the remission of our sins:

"He who did not spare his own Son but gave him up for us all, will he not also give us all things with him?" Romans 8:32

Furthermore we may well ask whether God would ever ask any man to express his love for him in a greater, more heart – rending way than God was ever disposed to show his love for men. When God asked Abraham to give his son, was this not surely a sign that a reciprocal demonstration of God's own love would follow in the gift of his Son for us? If not then we must conclude that one man gave a greater proof of his love of God than God has ever given for the whole of mankind in return. The thought is unthinkable. God would never ask any man to do more for him than he was willing to do for men himself. And the wondrous manifestation of his love in giving all he had in the death and resurrection of his Son Jesus Christ is proof sufficient of this. What better proof can we want of God's love for us? He has given his Son for us – one who proceeds from him – surely, then, he will give us all things with him. If he has, in his deep love, given us the greatest of all gifts, we must assuredly know that he will give us all lesser things as well. Furthermore we see that Abraham, a lowly creature, was prepared to give one like himself for the eternal God of the universe. It was his duty to obey any command God gave him. But what duty was imposed on the eternal Father of the heavens when he gave his Son – one like himself in every way for lowly men on earth? What other than infinite love could have motivated such action?

"For God so loved the world that he gave his only Son, that whoever believes in him should not perish but have eternal life." John 3:16

The Father did not stand idly by as men put his Son to an awful death, nor did he in an act of cruelty make an innocent victim of him. Oh no! Both the Father and the Son, in one united display of wondrous divine love for mankind, endured separation from each other to ensure that many men might be saved from an eternal separation in hell and be brought instead into eternal communion and glory with them. Nothing else but love could have endured the cross with all its horrors. Here we have a visible expression of God's love for us. In the gift of his Son he has given a full

manifestation of the depth of his love toward us:

"God shows his love for us in that while we were yet sinners Christ died for us." Romans 5:8

"In this the love of God was made manifest among us, that God sent his only Son into the world that we might live through him." 1 John 4:9

Surely men can now respond to God with unlimited I love in their hearts. Here is the glory of the Biblical revelation of the love of God in Jesus Christ. It is hardly surprising that the Koran has so little to say about the love of God when it denies that God gave his Son to redeem us from our sins. It has denied the greatest manifestation of this love

that could ever have been given by God to
men. As Jesus said:

"Greater love has no man than this, that a
man lay down his life for his friends." John
15:13
This is the greatest and most abiding form of
love – love that is as strong as death (Song
of Solomon 8:6) and cannot be overcome by
it. Such love was revealed in Jesus Christ
when he willingly laid down his life:

"When Jesus knew that his hour had come to
depart out of this world to the Father, having
loved his own who were in the world, he
loved them to the end." John 13:1

Here we have proof, not only of God's
inestimable love, but also of the fact that we
can depend on it forever. The true Christian
will never know a whit of God's wrath for he
is the eternal object of his immeasurable
love. The willing gift of his own Son was
perfect proof of the truth of this promise:

"I have loved you with an everlasting love."
Jeremiah 31:3

The cross of Jesus Christ was a magnificent
proof of the eternal love of both the Father

and the Son for mankind. Each was prepared to endure the loss of the other's presence – a circumstance which we cannot possibly estimate in our minds – so that we might never be lost. Not only so, but it is little wonder that after the death of Jesus and his resurrection to life again three days later God is only known as Father in the Holy Scriptures. This inexpressible gift shows us more than anything else ever could that God is indeed willing to become our Father. Through the cross he has redeemed all true believers in his Son to himself and has made possible even now the forgiveness of all our offences so that we might be transformed from children of wrath, which we are by nature, into children of God.

Not only has God become our Father through that which Jesus has done for us but, being the eternal Son from the Father, he has in fact revealed God himself to us as well:

"He who has seen me has seen the Father."
John 14:9
Therefore, not only do we see God's love made manifest in the gift of his Son Jesus Christ but we also have the glorious privilege of seeing in him the very personification of God's love. We are able,

in all that Jesus said and did, to obtain a very full knowledge of the love of God for us.

For no man ever loved as this man did. No deity of any other religion compares with him in his inexhaustible love for men. He lived for them and he died for them. His whole life was a living expression of love. He never once avenged himself on his enemies but loved them to such an extent that he even prayed on the cross for them in these words:

"Father, forgive them; for they know not what they do." Luke 23:34

He gave his disciples such a remarkable revelation of love in all that they saw him do in the three years he was with them that he was able to say to them on the last night that he was with them:

"A new commandment I give to you; that you love one another; even as I have loved you, that you also love one another." John 13:34

He ordered them to love each other as he had loved them. The world had never seen such depth of love as it saw in this man. Therefore, when he commanded his disciples to love one another in the same way that he had loved them, it was indeed a new commandment because the standard of this love was such as the world had never known before. Even others, who were not his disciples, when they saw how he grieved over the loss of one of his followers through an untimely death, said:

"See how he loved him!" John 11:36

We have, therefore, in the life of Jesus a wondrous example of the measure of the Father's love for us. As Ramsey, a former Archbishop of Canterbury, once put it so well: God is Christlike, and in him there is no un–Christlikeness at all. This is an incredible statement. Yet in no other way can the extent and wonder of God's love properly be expressed. The Father in heaven is the One whose image the Son bears (as we say in a proverb, "Like Father, like son") – therefore that love which was so great which the Son fully expressed in his life and death was nothing more or less than the Father's own love for us. Not only so, but the Son lived among men and was known by them. Surely, therefore, if the Father was revealed in the Son, then anyone who truly knew him knew his Father also (John 14:7). This means that we can not only have the magnificent privilege of beholding the love of God for us in the gift of his Son – a fact which demands the only reasonable response that men can give to this revelation of love, namely that we love him in return with all our hearts – but also that we can have the wondrous joy of actually KNOWING the love of God within our very own hearts. God himself has been revealed to us in Jesus Christ – by this we can not only perceive the expression of his love for us but also gain opportunity to actually experience that love within us. This leads us to our last consideration – the way by which God's love has become mutual between him and men – something which not only gives us potential to express heartfelt love for God but even to develop it to the full through the experience of his love for us in our own hearts.

5. Knowing God's Love through the Holy Spirit

Because God is our Father, we are able to have genuine love in our hearts toward him. Through his great work in his Son Jesus Christ we have seen how worthy he is of that love. But now, through the Holy Spirit (which is given to every true believer in Jesus Christ) we are able to actually experience his love for us within our hearts. As the Apostle Paul put it:
"Hope does not disappoint us, because God's love has been poured into our hearts through

the Holy Spirit which has been given to us."
Romans 5:5

What a wonderful statement this is. God's love has actually been poured into our hearts through the Holy Spirit which is given to every one at that moment that he turns and puts his faith in Jesus, seeking salvation in him alone. Not only do we behold God's love, therefore, for us in the gift of his Son but we can actually experience it within our own souls through the Holy Spirit who has been given to us. This principle of our adoption as children of God through Jesus Christ and our living experience of this relationship in the Holy Spirit was summed up by Paul in these words:

"But when the time had fully come, God sent forth his Son, born of a woman, born under the law, to redeem those who were under the law, so that we might receive adoption as sons. And because you are sons, God has sent the Spirit of his Son into our hearts, crying 'Abba! Father!'" Galatians 4:4-6

Here we have the climax of the revelation of God's love toward us. We have become children of God through the work of Jesus Christ whom God sent into the world to save us from our sins. But now, by sending the Spirit of his Son into our hearts, he has made us conscious right within our beings of our status before him. Not only are we children, we know we are children. We have been brought into the very same eternal, intimate communion that the Father and the Son have shared with each other from all eternity. Just as Jesus was able to call on his Father in heaven with an expression of intense intimacy, namely "Abba, Father" (Mark 14:36), so we have now been brought, by the mercies of God, into this same intimate relationship. ("Abba" is a Hebrew word which means "Father" but which is not translated into English because we have no corresponding word in our language which can possibly express the intimacy and closeness denoted by this word in Hebrew). Sufi Masters of old claimed to know the hundredth name of God (there are ninety-nine Al-Asma Al-Husna, "beautiful names" of God according to traditional Islam) but, in our view, if there is indeed another name of God which is missing from the ninety-nine, it is not the hundredth name but the first – namely this one: Father.

Within our very own hearts God has made us conscious of our relationship with him. As Paul put it:

"When we cry, 'Abba! Father!', it is the Spirit himself bearing witness with our spirit that we are children of God." Romans 8:15-26.

Christians, through the Holy Spirit, are able to call on God as their Father, a title which represents their relationship with him as no other really can.

The Holy Spirit within us has made us particularly aware of the fact that God is now our Father and we, therefore, call on him as such out of the deep knowledge of the love that he has for us. He is our Father in the very closest manner that he could be and through his Spirit he has impressed this fact very surely on us. All this has been done through the redemption which he set forth and accomplished through his Son Jesus Christ. By dying for our sins to cleanse us from all evil Jesus has made it possible for us to fully enjoy this new relationship.

"For through him we both have access in one Spirit to the Father." Ephesians 2:16 Through him the Christian has obtained access to this grace in which he now stands. The love of the Father, made manifest in the Son, has now become our own personal possession through the Holy Spirit which he has given us. Jesus himself urged his disciples to strengthen and develop this love in their hearts:

"As the Father has loved me, so have I loved you; abide in my love." John 15:9

We cannot tell how deeply the Father, through the Son, desires that we should know this love in our own hearts. When Jesus prayed to his Father in heaven on the last night he was with his disciples he made it clear that his whole purpose in coming to earth was to make this love real to them: "I made known to them thy name, and I will make it known, that the love with which thou hast loved me may be in them, and I in them."
John 17:26

Ten days after the ascension of Jesus to heaven his disciples first received the Holy Spirit. From that day the personal knowledge of God's love has become available to all men. All who turn to him in faith and love through his Son Jesus Christ will not fail to discover the joy of salvation that accompanies the consciousness of this love in our hearts. As Jesus said to his disciples again on the last night he was with them:
"For the Father himself loves you, because you have loved me and have believed that I came from the Father." John 16:27

Here, then, we find the final proof of God's love toward men. By becoming our Father he has made it possible for us to express genuine love toward him without fear of his wrath in our hearts. He has shown his love to us in a remarkable way by giving his Son Jesus Christ to redeem us from our sins. By giving us his Spirit he has made it openly possible for that love to become thoroughly mutual between him and us. In turn we are now able to truly love him with all our hearts, souls and minds. He is worthy of such love and has made it possible for us to express it to the fullest.

What will a man offer to God in return for such love? Can he give anything to compare with it? After all that God has done for us, can we honestly believe that we can merit favor with him through our own half hearted, feeble religious efforts?

"Many waters cannot quench love, neither can floods drown it. If a man offered for love all the wealthy of his house, it would be utterly scorned." Song of Solomon 8:7

God does not want from sinners their pilgrimages, prayers and religious devotions and various ecclesiastical duties mixed through and through with the evils they think and do every day. He cannot endure

iniquity and solemn assembly (Isaiah 1:13).
If we hope to obtain his good pleasure by
anything we do on our own account, while
we casually overlook the sins we commit,
we scorned utterly the love he has revealed
to us.

The Father wants none of your efforts – he
wants YOU. He desires that you respond to
this glorious manifestation of his love. This
wondrous revelation of the love of the
Father, Son and Holy Spirit has been given
to the world so that God may obtain from us
that which alone is acceptable to him. He
wants us to become his children and to love
him with all our hearts, souls and minds.
Any good work of grace or religious deed
that flows out of such love is acceptable to
him. But no work other than this can ever
merit acceptance with him.

So many, with no certainty of forgiveness,
offer religious works to God with the hope
of thereby obtaining his approval and
forgiveness. But how can our paltry efforts,
wrapped in the multitude of sins that we
commit every day, ever possibly merit his
approval?

God has provided a better and more certain
way of gaining his commendation. He who
turns away from his own works and trusts in
Jesus Christ instead obtains forgiveness of
his sins and newness of life. The true

Christian dies in the assured knowledge of God's love and favor. Will you not rather turn to him who can save your soul? God stretches out his hand to you in eternal love – will you not clasp it and obtain the salvation God is freely offering you? Will you not believe in his Son who died for you so that you can become a child of God? Will you not receive the Holy Spirit so that, like an orphan, you can experience his warm embrace and know in your heart that God is your Father?

"That which we have seen and heard we proclaim also to you, so that you may have fellowship with us; and our fellowship is with the Father and with his Son Jesus Christ." 1 John 1:3

Salvation In Islam and Christianity
What is Original Sin?
Romans 5:12, "Therefore, just as through one man sin entered the world, and death through sin, and thus death spread to all men, because all sinned;"
Because Adam and Eve sinned, sin came in this world. That's what we see in this world, full of sin and violence. Before sin came in this world, Adam and Eve never knew any sin nor violence. They never knew what death and curse was. They never knew what it was to sweat and do hard work. They

never knew what tears or sorrow was. They were in perfect peace and happiness. They had fellowship with God.

But only one sin made every difference. If we read in Genesis Chapter 3, we can see that not only did God curse Adam, Eve and the serpent but He also cursed the ground. Genesis 3:17 - 19 Then to Adam He said, "Because you have heeded the voice of your wife, and have eaten from the tree of which I commanded you, saying, 'You shall not eat of it': "Cursed is the ground for your sake; In toil you shall eat of it All the days of your life. Both thorns and thistles it shall bring forth for you, And you shall eat the herb of the field. In the sweat of your face you shall eat bread Till you return to the ground, For out of it you were taken; For dust you are, And to dust you shall return."

These verses clearly says that because of the sin of Adam and Eve, thorn and thistles started growing. Men had to do hard work for his living and women had to go through pain in childbirth etc. And more than this, both Adam and Eve lost the fellowship of God. They were alienated from God and His presence. They died spiritually. Today, the same blood is flowing through us, the same corrupted blood. That's why David says in Psalms 51:5, "Behold, I was brought forth in iniquity, And in sin my mother conceived me." David describes here about the sinful nature that we got from Adam and Eve. That is the reason we bend toward evil and whatever comes in our heart is evil. But the same Bible that says about the sinful nature of us, says about the redemption of our sins.

If we read in the Koran and the Bible we can see that the Koran also says the same thing: Sura 7:22. So by deceit he brought about their fall: when they tasted of the tree, their shame became manifest to them, and they began to sew together the leaves of the garden over their bodies. And their Lord called unto them: "Did I not forbid you that tree, and tell you that Satan was an avowed enemy unto you?"
Sura 7:23. They said: "Our Lord! We have wronged our own souls: If thou forgive us not and bestow not upon us Thy Mercy, we shall certainly be lost."
Sura 7:24. ((Allah)) said: "Get ye down. With enmity between yourselves. On earth will be your dwelling-place and your means of livelihood,– for a time."
Sura 7:25. He said: "Therein shall ye live, and therein shall ye die; but from it shall ye be taken out (at last)."
Sura 7:26. "O ye Children of Adam! We have bestowed raiment upon you to cover your shame, as well as to be an adornment to

you. But the raiment of righteousness,– that is the best. Such are among the Signs of Allah, that they may receive admonition!" All these verses say about the fall of Adam and repentance and forgiveness of sin. These verses also say that because of the sin of Adam, curse and death came in this world. Their shame became manifest to them and they started to sew cloths for them. And further we read that God gave them the raiment to cover their shame, as well as to be an adornment to them.

And the same thing Bible says in Genesis 3:21, "Also for Adam and his wife the LORD God made tunics of skin, and clothed them."

From where the skin came? Certainly God sacrificed an animal to cover the shame of Adam and Eve. The same thing Jesus did on the cross. To cover our shame and shameful act, to cover our sins and consequences of sin, to cover and take our guilt and sinful nature from us, He died on the cross. He shed His precious blood on the cruel cross for me and for you so that we may never be in shame and sin.

We Need a Savior

Because we are born in sin that's why we bent toward evil and sin. David says in Psalms 51:5, "Behold, I was brought forth in iniquity, And in sin my mother conceived me." We can not come out from our sinful nature by our good deeds or by our own efforts. Yes, we need a Savior, we need a Messiah who can rescue us from our sins. Genesis 3:19, "In the sweat of your face you shall eat bread till you return to the ground, For out of it you were taken; For dust you are, And to dust you shall return."

This verse says, "Dust you are" it means they were created by dust as the Bible says in Gen 2:7, "And the LORD God formed man of the dust of the ground, and breathed into his nostrils the breath of life; and man became a living being." And the verse in Genesis 3:17 says that, "And to dust you shall return." This verse clearly says that man/woman will die (they will return to dust). And more than this, Bible says about SPIRITUAL DEATH. We are made up of 3 parts: 1. Soul, 2. Body, 3. Mind.

So when God said to Adam, "You will surely die." then He meant that, You will die spiritually. That's what happened in the garden of Eden. Adam and Eve sinned but they did not die immediately (physically) but the moment they sinned they died spiritually. Their soul became dead and they separated from God because there is no sin in God and God can not be with those who sin.

Yes, Adam sinned and brought death and curse in this world, but Jesus came and died on the cross, He shed His precious blood to save us from eternal death, tears, sorrow, pain and curse. He came down to give us eternal life. We can receive this wonderful life which Adam and Eve had in the Garden of Eden – a life full of blessings, a life full of peace and joy. If you have not yet received this life, today is the day of salvation. Invite Jesus into your life and your life will never be the same again.

My dear friend, we are all under curse that's why we see this much misery and pain in this world and if we want to come out from our sins, there is only one way, i.e., the blood of Jesus. Jesus Himself said in Matthew 26:28, "For this is My blood of the new covenant, which is shed for many for the remission of sins."

And Jesus said in John 8:34-36, Jesus answered them, "Most assuredly, I say to you, whoever commits sin is a slave of sin. And a slave does not abide in the house forever, but a son abides forever. Therefore if the Son makes you free, you shall be free indeed."

How can we get Salvation?

1. Realize that you are sinner:

1 John 1:8, "If we say that we have no sin,

we deceive ourselves, and the truth is not in us."

2. Confess from your mouth:

1 John 1:9 "If we confess our sins, He is faithful and just to forgive us our sins and to cleanse us from all unrighteousness." And also the Bible says in

Romans 10:9 that if you confess with your mouth the Lord Jesus and believe in your heart that God has raised Him from the dead, you will be saved.

3. Repent from your sins:

Acts 3:19 "Repent therefore and be converted, that your sins may be blotted out, so that times of refreshing may come from the presence of the Lord."

4. Accept Jesus as your Lord and Savior:

By faith accept Jesus as your Lord and Savior of your life and invite Him in your life. When a person does this his/her life changes and he/she becomes a new creation.

5. New creation: 2 Corinthians 5:17

"Therefore, if anyone is in Christ, he is a new creation; old things have passed away; behold, all things have become new."

6. Promise of eternal life:

John 5:24 "Most assuredly, I say to you, he who hears My word and believes in Him who sent Me has everlasting life, and shall not come into judgment, but has passed from death into life."

Mohammad Wasn't Sure about Salvation
Jabir reported that the Prophet of Islam said:
"No good works of yours can ever secure
heaven for you, nor can they save you from
hell – not even me, without the grace of
God."
Abu Huraira related that when the verse,
"Cause thy near relatives to fear," was
revealed to the Prophet of Islam, the Prophet
arose and began to proclaim: "Oh people of
the Quraysh, and you sons of Abdul Manaf,
and you Abbas, son of Abdul Muttalib, and
you, Safiyyah my aunt, I cannot save you
from the punishment of the Day of
Resurrection. Take care of yourself, O my
daughter Fatimah; you may use my
property, but I cannot save you from God.
Take care of yourself" (Bukhari).
Abu Huraira reported that the Prophet of
Islam said: "No one of you will enter
Paradise through his good works." They
said: "Not even you, O Apostle of God?"
"Not even I," he replied, "unless God cover
me with His grace and mercy. Therefore be
strong, and
morning and evening, nay every moment,
try to do good."
Mohammad's prayer asking forgiveness:
Volume 1, Book 12, Number 711:
Narrated Abu Huraira: Allah's Apostle used
to keep silent between the Takbir and the

recitation of Koran and that interval of silence used to be a short one. I said to the Prophet "May my parents be sacrificed for you! What do you say in the pause between Takbir and recitation?" The Prophet said, "I say, 'Allahumma, ba'id baini wa baina khatayaya kama ba'adta baina-l-mashriqi wa-l-maghrib. Allahumma, naqqim min khatayaya kama yunaqqa-ththawbu-l-abyadu mina-ddanas. Allahumma, ighsil khatayaya bil-ma'i wa-th-thalji wal-barad (O Allah! Set me apart from my sins (faults) as the East and West are set apart from each other and clean me from sins as a white garment is cleaned of dirt (after thorough washing). O Allah! Wash off my sins with water, snow and hail.)"

There is no Salvation in Islam
Allah Promised hell for his followers:
Al-Imran (The Family of Imran)
Sura 3:185, "Every soul shall have a taste of death: And only on the Day of Judgment shall you be paid your full recompense. Only he who is saved far from the Fire and admitted to the Garden will have attained the object (of Life): For the life of this world is but goods and chattels of deception."

This Suras from Koran very clearly says that after death everyone will go to hell fire then judgment. When a person went to hell fire then how and why it is possible that he/she

214

can come out from hell fire and go to paradise... no way... This verse does not say anything about eternal life. This verse very clearly says that every believer in Allah is tasting death means they did not get the life while Jesus promised eternal life and heaven as we read in John 10:10:
"The thief does not come except to steal, and to kill, and to destroy. I have come that they may have life, and that they may have it more abundantly."
And also every soul is going to hell fire till the day of judgment means they are not reaching heaven. So of course Allah promised hell fire for his believers. I said "no way" for coming out from the hell fire and go to heaven. There is no chance to go to heaven once you go to hell fire . . . But yes, Jesus can save you when you are still in this world as He said in John 3:15 "that whoever believes in Him should not perish but have eternal life."

John 3:16 "For God so loved the world that He gave His only begotten Son, that whoever believes in Him should not perish but have everlasting life"
How a person can save himself/herself from hell fire when he/she is already in hell fire? And this verse says that they will be there till the time of Day of Judgment. Do you

think a person who is already in hell fire will get a seat in heaven after judgment? Judgment is a day when people get their sentence and verdict . . . no reward my friend that day.

Allah promised hell fire for his followers but contrary to it Jesus promised heaven for His followers.

APPENDIX F

The Reformer Muhammad

God always raises up someone from among their own people to bring about reformation when that people or nation is faced with the sin of idolatry. I said it once and I declare it again that Muhammad was raised up to bring reformation to the seed of Ishmael, and the Koran gives us a picture of this in SURA 39:17, "And they who avoid the worship of idols and turn to God. For them is Good News, so give Good News to my servants." Here guidance is declared to the seed of Ishmael concerning the worship of idols. Ishmael's seed worshiped more than 365 idols, and here God promises Good News or Blessings to those who will avoid or turn away from idol worship. Notice what the next verse says in SURA 39:18, "Who listens to the word, then follows it. Such are they whom God will guide and such are the men of understanding."

There is too much argument over whether the Bible and the Koran are speaking of the same God, or whether the God in the Koran is the same God, which is in the Bible. There is much truth in the Koran that is the same truth as mentioned in the Holy Bible. I believe that a lot of so-called scholars argue and seek to keep confusion going on when God Himself is not the author of confusion.

There is enough truth in the Koran that points to the Bible to save one billion Muslims if it is done so by the will of God, and Godly compassion within the ones who are called to do such a work as this. The fact remains that God has promised to save and bless the seed of Ishmael. Some men amaze me because of their egos, and because of men's egos. I believe that in these last days God will use women to get behind the right men with the vision of God, and help bring God's promise into a reality. The truth is that God's ultimate aim is to bring man and woman back to the place He originally and ultimately planned for all humanity, and that again is in His image and likeness. It is when we get back to where God originally intended for us to be that all such things as time and space will be no more. He that has an ear, let him hear what the spirit has said.

From the beginning of time (Genesis) God declared the end, or what will happen in the end of this world, as we now know it. All of us who are born into Christ, and His kingdom, must experience what Joseph experienced among his brothers. We must experience this on our way to the Palace, a place of authority and kingdom prosperity. The making of a Godly man and a Godly woman is somewhat painful simply because of the lessons that must be learned in order to rule in righteousness.

The answer to the Muslim religion is that they must be born again. The answer to all of the human beings who are seeking a relationship with the Almighty God, is that we ALL MUST BE BORN AGAIN! The born again life is the first step to returning humanity back to God's original plan. In the beginning when God said, "Let us make man in our own image (the root word of imagination) and our own likeness."

We have literally been reading and trying to understand the Bible backwards. The great prophet Isaiah points us to the right understanding and way of God. God said through the prophet Isaiah, "I will make the crooked places straight." Isaiah is speaking of clearing up what was messed up.

ISAIAH 46:9, "Remember the former things of old." Here God is saying to us who are seeking truth, Use Your Imagination! God goes on to say, "There is none like me." Now in verse 10 He tells us what makes Him different. "Declaring the end from the beginning." Let's stop right here. God says to those who have an ear to hear what makes Him like no one else is that He declares the end from the beginning. When was the beginning? If I can find the beginning, I will actually see the end. The word Genesis means The Beginning, so what we see and read in Genesis is actually a picture of the end of time. Approximately 6001 years in time.

We are approximately 6004 years from Genesis chapter one. This is what practicing Christians must begin to understand. Satan is in the garden of the human spirit and must be cast out NOW! This man Adam who is known as the first Adam, was a picture of the human family, who would enter into the new Garden of Eden (The Kingdom of God), at the end of the world that existed under Satan's 6000–year rule. The reason why the devil could not kill me on October 20, 2003 in a potentially deadly car accident was because his ruler-ship was finished.

This is the hour that God spoke of from GENESIS when He said, "Let us make man." God was declaring the end from the beginning.

Adam in Genesis, aborted his potential to be like God, or godlike. What I have learned and witnessed, even in the church, is that many Christians abort their potential because they get stuck in man-made laws and traditions in the church. Many of the church leaders have made the church their ownership, and have kicked Christ out. What we must understand, as I have said in meetings across the nation, is that the church is only the womb that birthed us, and from the church we are to grow into Strength, Vision, Faith, Love and Power. Let me explain it this way, as I have come to understand this from God Himself. There were three feast days a year according to the Hebrew calendar. The first of these days was called, and is still called, Passover. The second Holy day was called Pentecost, and the third day is called the Feast of Tabernacles. Each day is progressive. They actually represent the three stages of our spiritual growth. From Passover the blood covers us, and through Pentecost we are filled with the Holy Ghost through our new birth, but then we actually move on into the

Feast of Tabernacles, which is into the presence of God, where we are deputized to do the works of God. Some, and most members of the church do not wish to go any further than a church religious ceremony. They are content with Sunday morning, Sunday night and Wednesday or Thursday night Bible classes. They are not taught that there is another level or worship after Pentecost, which is the Feast of Tabernacles where we actually enter into the presence of God, and supernatural things happen in, through and for us.

There are people in the church who cannot see the Muslim world saved, and sanctified through the power of the gospel, in which we preach. Here I am on worldwide television saying, we will teach them from their own book which is 95% Bible. This kind of knowledge did not come to me sitting on church pews, but it came to me while I listened to the Spirit of God in intimate fellowship with Him.

God created Adam in Genesis, and in Isaiah He recreates us all over again for a greater purpose. ISAIAH 43:7, "Even everyone who is called by my name for I have created him for my glory, (or for my presence) I have formed him; yes, I have made him."

This, beloved is not Adam. This is you and I who will usher in a New World called The Kingdom of God. ISAIAH 51:16, "I have put my words in your mouth, and I have covered you in the shadow of my hand, that I may plant the heavens and lay the foundations of the earth and say unto those who are in my kingdom you are mine." II PETER 2:9, " For you are a royal priesthood and chosen generation a holy kingdom, God's own people that you might show forth the praises of Him who has called you out of Darkness into His marvelous light."

The Kingdom People

Here we are 6004 years from the book of
Genesis, and most Christians, and those who
profess to know Christ, are totally unaware
of the time, and what we must do from this
time, that is in direct relationship with our
Divine Destiny. There exists in the Bible,
two creations of The Heavens and The
Earth, and two creations of man. Both of
the first creations have fallen, and were
pictures of the intent of Almighty God, but
the first was temporal, while the last creation
of the Heavens and The Earth and man, are
Eternal. We don't die, we multiply.

Again, look at the eagle-eyed prophet, Isaiah
47:3. "Even everyone who is called by my
name for I have created him for my glory,
yea I have formed him." God spoke in the
past before Christ came to the Earth about
the prophetic future of man. This man, or
this generation would not occur in its
fullness until 2001. The year of the
beginning of God's Kingdom on Earth. A
Kingdom that will be able to bring the seed
of Ishmael into The Kingdom of God. We
are three years in the Days of The Kingdom
of God. Out of all the smoke, out of all the
chaos of 911, the birth of God's Kingdom

occurred and is now being manifested from the shores of North America.

The only problem in Christianity, along with much Theology, is that it has closed the minds and eyes to this Powerful Truth. Isn't it strange that America thought that the computer crash and water and electrical power outage would all occur in the year 2000, but one year later the whole world took a total turn after 9-11-2001. Many had predicted the end of the world as we know it would occur in 2000, but in reality it was September 11, 2001 that he whole world took a total change, and now Terrorism, as it is called, has destroyed and threatened the whole world to the core. DANIEL 12:1, "Declare that at that time God's people will be raised up or delivered." The power to turn this whole situation around is not in a gun, a ship, or a bomb, but the thing that God will use to turn this world into a peaceful glorious world is a word from His people in The Kingdom of God. Now we can understand ROMANS 8:19, "For the eager hope of the creation awaiteth for the manifestation of the sons of God."

We are all awaiting the return of Jesus the Holy Messiah. Not Moses and not Muhammad, but Jesus the Holy Messiah.

Continue at verse 21, "Because the creation itself also shall be delivered from the bondage of death (the bondage of death occurred in Genesis) into the glorious liberty of the children of God." The children of God are the children of The Kingdom of God. EZEKIEL 37:22, " And I will make them one nation in the land upon the mountain of Israel and one King shall be King to them all (Jesus The Messiah), and they shall no more be two nations anymore at all." Verse 23, "Neither shall they defile themselves anymore with idols." Muhammad came over 1400 years ago to the Arab world to reform them from their idolatry, and from as this verse proclaim from their detestable things.

God is about to create divine favor for us from the Islamic leaders, for many Imams of the Islamic faith have said to me personally that the true Muslims know that we are all awaiting the return of Jesus the Holy Messiah, and not Moses and not Muhammad. The book of Ezekiel clearly says that Ishmael and Isaac will both become one nation. How will it happen, and when will it happen? Most of the people who read this book will probably say, I think that this man has not seen the news lately, or maybe he doesn't read the newspapers anymore, but in the midst of what seem to be impossible, it looks very different to those of us who know the time and what Almighty God is about to do. The truth of the Gospel is moving throughout the world. Millions of those who are of the seed of Ishmael are every minute receiving Christ as their Redeemer. The word has gone out and the Holy Spirit is moving and is drawing the seed of Ishmael closer and closer to The Kingdom of God.

I say unto all of you, open up your eyes and see it, and open up your mouth and declare it for it has been written in DANIEL 2:44, "And in the days of these kings shall the God of Heaven set up a Kingdom which shall never be destroyed, and this kingdom shall not be left to other people, but his Kingdom shall consume all of those kingdoms, and it shall stand forever." The kingdoms of which are now known as the Middle East will be consumed by the Kingdom of God and His Christ, and it will rule and abide forever. IT SHALL BE DONE!

APPENDIX G

The promises of God in Isaiah for your spiritual enlightenment

I personally wanted to share with you how I believe the Lord has blessed my family and this wonderful ministry since I came out of the nation of Islam and the power found in His Word and most of all his promises. 2 Peter 1:4 says that the Lord has given unto us exceeding great and precious promises that through these we might become partakers of his divine nature. Do we understand the power of a promise from God? And do we understand just what authority a promise from God gives us?

I have proclaimed throughout the world what I believe has changed thousands of lives, especially mine. Adam fell from his lofty potential because he did not have a promise from God, and the same holds true with Noah. But the reason why Abraham was so blessed and successful was because instead God commanded Abraham to be fruitful and multiply. God made Abraham a promise in Genesis 17:6 stating, "I will make thee exceeding fruitful and I will make nations of thee and kings shall come out of thee." You and I have the potential to reveal the Lord our God in this earthen human form like never before, to be totally invincible. Please read and eat these promises and see the glory of the Lord in you like never before.

Kingdom blessings always,
Dr. Jeremiah Cummings
Isai 4:5 And the LORD will create upon every dwelling place of mount Zion, and upon her assemblies, a cloud and smoke by day, and the shining of a flaming fire by night: for upon all the glory [shall be] a defence. 6 And there shall be a tabernacle for a shadow in the daytime from the heat, and for a place of refuge, and for a covert from storm and from rain.

Isai 11:6 The wolf also shall dwell with the lamb, and the leopard shall lie down with the kid; and the calf and the young lion and the fatling together; and a little child shall lead them. 7 And the cow and the bear shall feed; their young ones shall lie down together: and the lion shall eat straw like the ox. 8 And the sucking child shall play on the hole of the asp, and the weaned child shall put his hand on the cockatrice' den. 9 They shall not hurt nor destroy in all my holy mountain: for the earth shall be full of the

knowledge of the LORD, as the waters
cover the sea.

Isai 25:8 He will swallow up death in
victory; and the Lord GO
D will wipe away tears from off all faces;
and the rebuke of his people shall he take
away from off all the earth: for the LORD
hath spoken [it].

Isai 26:3 Thou wilt keep [him] in perfect
peace, [whose] mind [is] stayed [on thee]:
because he trusteth in thee.

Isai 33:16 He shall dwell on high: his place
of defence [shall be] the munitions of rocks:
bread shall be given him; his waters [shall
be] sure.

Isai 33:21 But there the glorious LORD
[will be] unto us a place of broad rivers
[and] streams; wherein shall go no galley
with oars, neither shall gallant ship pass
thereby. 22 For the LORD [is] our judge, the
LORD [is] our lawgiver, the LORD [is] our
king; he will save us.

Isai 33:24 And the inhabitant shall not say, I
am sick: the people that dwell therein [shall
be] forgiven [their] iniquity.

Isai 35:10 And the ransomed of the LORD shall return, and come to Zion with songs and everlasting joy upon their heads: they shall obtain joy and gladness, and sorrow and sighing shall flee away.

Isai 40:10 Behold, the Lord GOD will come with strong [hand], and his arm shall rule for him: behold, his reward [is] with him, and his work before him. 11 He shall feed his flock like a shepherd: he shall gather the lambs with his arm, and carry [them] in his bosom, [and] shall gently lead those that are with young.

Isai 40:29 He giveth power to the faint; and to [them that have] no might he increaseth strength.

Isai 40:31 But they that wait upon the LORD shall renew [their] strength; they shall mount up with wings as eagles; they shall run, and not be weary; [and] they shall walk, and not faint.

Isai 41:10 Fear thou not; for I [am] with thee: be not dismayed; for I [am] thy God: I will strengthen thee; yea, I will help thee; yea, I will uphold thee with the right hand of my righteousness. 11 Behold, all they that were incensed against thee shall be ashamed and confounded: they shall be as nothing; and they that strive with thee shall perish.

Isai 41:13 For I the LORD thy God will hold thy right hand, saying unto thee, Fear not; I will help thee.

Isai 43:2 When thou passest through the waters, I [will be] with thee; and through the rivers, they shall not overflow thee: when thou walkest through the fire, thou shalt not be burned; neither shall the flame kindle upon thee.

Isai 44:2 Thus saith the LORD that made thee, and formed thee from the womb, [which] will help thee; Fear not, O Jacob, my servant; and thou, Jesurun, whom I have chosen. 3 For I will pour water upon him that is thirsty, and floods upon the dry ground: I will pour my spirit upon thy seed, and my blessing upon thine offspring:

Isai 49:9 That thou mayest say to the prisoners, Go forth; to them that [are] in darkness, Shew yourselves. They shall feed in the ways, and their pastures [shall be] in all high places. 10 They shall not hunger nor thirst; neither shall the heat nor sun smite them: for he that hath mercy on them shall lead them, even by the springs of water shall he guide them. 11 And I will make all my mountains a way, and my highways shall be exalted. 12 Behold, these shall come from far: and, lo, these from the north and from the west; and these from the land of Sinim. Isai 50:7 For the Lord GOD will help me; therefore shall I not be confounded: therefore have I set my face like a flint, and I know that I shall not be ashamed. 8 [He is] near that justifieth me; who will contend with me? let us stand together: who [is] mine adversary? let him come near to me. 9 Behold, the Lord GOD will help me; who [is] he [that] shall condemn me? lo, they all shall wax old as a garment; the moth shall eat them up.

Isai 51:11 Therefore the redeemed of the LORD shall return, and come with singing unto Zion; and everlasting joy [shall be] upon their head: they shall obtain gladness and joy; [and] sorrow and mourning shall flee away.

Isai 54:1 Sing, O barren, thou [that] didst not bear; break forth into singing, and cry aloud, thou [that] didst not travail with child: for more [are] the children of the desolate than the children of the married wife, saith the LORD. 2 Enlarge the place of thy tent, and let them stretch forth the curtains of thine habitations: spare not, lengthen thy cords, and strengthen thy stakes; 3 For thou shalt break forth on the right hand and on the left; and thy seed shall inherit the Gentiles, and make the desolate cities to be inhabited. 4 Fear not; for thou shalt not be ashamed: neither be thou confounded; for thou shalt not be put to shame: for thou shalt forget the shame of thy youth, and shalt not remember the reproach of thy widowhood any more. 5 For thy Maker [is] thine husband; the LORD of hosts [is] his name; and thy Redeemer the Holy One of Israel; The God of the whole earth shall he be called. 6 For the LORD hath called thee as a woman forsaken and grieved in spirit, and a wife of youth, when thou wast refused, saith thy God. 7 For a small moment have I forsaken thee; but with great mercies will I gather thee. 8 In a little wrath I hid my face from thee for a moment; but with everlasting kindness will I have mercy on thee, saith the LORD thy Redeemer. 9 For this [is as] the waters of Noah unto me: for [as] I have sworn that the waters of Noah should no more go over the earth; so have I sworn that I would not be wroth with thee, nor rebuke thee. 10 For the mountains shall depart, and the hills be removed; but my kindness shall not depart from thee, neither shall the covenant of my peace be removed, saith the LORD that hath mercy on thee. 11 O thou afflicted, tossed with tempest, [and] not comforted, behold, I will lay thy stones with fair colours, and lay thy foundations with sapphires. 12 And I will make thy windows of agates, and thy gates of carbuncles, and all thy borders of pleasant stones. 13 And all thy children [shall be] taught of the LORD; and great [shall be] the peace of thy children. 14 In righteousness shalt thou be established: thou shalt be far from oppression; for thou shalt not fear: and from terror; for it shall not come near thee. 15 Behold, they shall surely gather together, [but] not by me: whosoever shall gather together against thee shall fall for thy sake. 16 Behold, I have created the smith that bloweth the coals in the fire, and that bringeth forth an instrument for his work; and I have created the waster to destroy. 17 No weapon that is formed against thee shall prosper; and every tongue [that] shall rise against thee in judgment thou shalt condemn. This [is] the heritage of the servants of the LORD, and their righteousness [is] of me, saith the LORD.

Isai 56:2 Blessed [is] the man [that] doeth this, and the son of man [that] layeth hold on it; that keepeth the sabbath from polluting it, and keepeth his hand from doing any evil. 3 Neither let the son of the stranger, that hath joined himself to the LORD, speak, saying, The LORD hath utterly separated me from his people: neither let the eunuch say, Behold, I [am] a dry tree. 4 For thus saith the LORD unto the eunuchs that keep my sabbaths, and choose [the things] that please me, and take hold of my covenant; 5 Even unto them will I give in mine house and within my walls a place and a name better than of sons and of daughters: I will give them an everlasting name, that shall not be cut off. 6 Also the sons of the stranger, that join themselves to the LORD, to serve him, and to love the name of the LORD, to be his servants, every one that keepeth the sabbath from polluting it, and taketh hold of my covenant; 7 Even them will I bring to my holy mountain, and make them joyful in my house of prayer: their burnt offerings and their sacrifices [shall be] accepted upon mine altar; for mine house shall be called an house of prayer for all people. 8 The Lord GOD which gathereth the outcasts of Israel saith, Yet will I gather [others] to him, beside those that are gathered unto him.

Isai 57:1 The righteous perisheth, and no man layeth [it] to heart: and merciful men [are] taken away, none considering that the righteous is taken away from the evil [to come]. 2 He shall enter into peace: they shall rest in their beds, [each one] walking [in] his uprightness.

Isai 58:8 Then shall thy light break forth as the morning, and thine health shall spring forth speedily: and thy righteousness shall go before thee; the glory of the LORD shall be thy rereward. 9 Then shalt thou call, and the LORD shall answer; thou shalt cry, and he shall say, Here I [am]. If thou take away from the midst of thee the yoke, the putting forth of the finger, and speaking vanity; 10 And [if] thou draw out thy soul to the hungry, and satisfy the afflicted soul; then shall thy light rise in obscurity, and thy darkness [be] as the noonday: 11 And the LORD shall guide thee continually, and satisfy thy soul in drought, and make fat thy bones: and thou shalt be like a watered garden, and like a spring of water, whose waters fail not. 12 And [they that shall be] of thee shall build the old waste places: thou shalt raise up the foundations of many generations; and thou shalt be called, The repairer of the breach, The restorer of paths to dwell in. 13 If thou turn away thy foot from the sabbath, [from] doing thy pleasure on my holy day; and call the sabbath a delight, the holy of the LORD, honourable; and shalt honour him, not doing thine own ways, nor finding thine own pleasure, nor speaking [thine own] words: 14 Then shalt thou delight thyself in the LORD; and I will cause thee to ride upon the high places of the earth, and feed thee with the heritage of Jacob thy father: for the mouth of the LORD hath spoken [it].

Isai 59:20 And the Redeemer shall come to Zion, and unto them that turn from transgression in Jacob, saith the LORD. 21 As for me, this [is] my covenant with them, saith the LORD; My spirit that [is] upon thee, and my words which I have put in thy mouth, shall not depart out of thy mouth, nor out of the mouth of thy seed, nor out of the mouth of thy seed's seed, saith the LORD, from henceforth and for ever.

Isai 64:4 For since the beginning of the world [men] have not heard, nor perceived by the ear, neither hath the eye seen, O God, beside thee, [what] he hath prepared for him that waiteth for him.

Isai 65:13 Therefore thus saith the Lord GOD, Behold, my servants shall eat, but ye shall be hungry: behold, my servants shall drink, but ye shall be thirsty: behold, my servants shall rejoice, but ye shall be ashamed: 14 Behold, my servants shall sing for joy of heart, but ye shall cry for sorrow of heart, and shall howl for vexation of spirit.

Isai 65:17 For, behold, I create new heavens and a new earth: and the former shall not be remembered, nor come into mind. 18 But be ye glad and rejoice for ever [in that] which I create: for, behold, I create Jerusalem a rejoicing, and her people a joy. 19 And I will rejoice in Jerusalem, and joy in my people: and the voice of weeping shall be no more heard in her, nor the voice of crying. 20 There shall be no more thence an infant of days, nor an old man that hath not filled his days: for the child shall die an hundred years old; but the sinner [being] an hundred years old shall be accursed. 21 And they shall build houses, and inhabit [them]; and they shall plant vineyards, and eat the fruit of them. 22 They shall not build, and another inhabit; they shall not plant, and another eat: for as the days of a tree [are] the days of my people, and mine elect shall long enjoy the work of their hands. 23 They shall not labour in vain, nor bring forth for trouble; for they [are] the seed of the blessed of the LORD, and their offspring with them. 24 And it shall come to pass, that before they call, I will answer; and while they are yet speaking, I will hear. 25 The wolf and the lamb shall feed together, and the lion shall eat straw like the bullock: and dust [shall be] the serpent's meat. They shall not hurt nor destroy in all my holy mountain, saith the LORD.

Isai 66:13 As one whom his mother comforteth, so will I comfort you; and ye shall be comforted in Jerusalem. 14 And when ye see [this], your heart shall rejoice, and your bones shall flourish like an herb: and the hand of the LORD shall be known toward his servants, and [his] indignation toward his enemies.

Worldwide International Campaign for Christ &
WKGN TELVIVION
P.O. Box 677276, Orlando FL 32867
866.924.WICC   wicctv.org

Product Order Form

Name: _____

Mailing Address: _____

City, ST & Zip: _____

Email Address: _____

Please indicate the type (VHS, CD, DVD)

Product #	Qty	Type	Description	Total Cost
12BK		Book	Reaching For The World	$
29			Mind & Mouth Determine Your Destiny	$
31			You Ain't Seen Nothing Yet	$
28			I Am Free	$
25			Power of the Promise	$
52			The Mystery of Man on the Sixth Day	$
21MCD (Music)		CD-DVD	Harvest Time For the Heirs of God	$

All VHS/DVD & Book are $20 each, CD's are $15 each, include $4 per item for shipping & handling. **Method of Payment** *(Be a good steward and operate with integrity and excellence. Your check will be electronically deposited so make sure funds are available in your account)* **You may also order online at www.wicctv.org.**

(Please Print Clearly)

Check/MO # _____   Check/MO Amt _____

Billing Name: _____

Credit Card _____ Mastercard _____ Visa _____ AMEX

Card # _____ Exp Date: _____

Total Amt: _____ Signature: _____

241

WorldWide International Campaign for Christ
P.O. Box 677276, Orlando FL 32867
866.924.WICC wicctv.org

Product Order Form

Name: _____

Mailing Address: _____

City, ST & Zip: _____

Email Address: _____

Please indicate the type (VHS, CD, DVD)

Product #	Qty	Type	Description	Cost
12BK		Book	Reaching For The World	$
29			Mind & Mouth Determine Your Destiny	$
31			Give Me This Water	$
28			I Am Free	$
25			Power of the Promise	$
53		CD-DVD	The Glory of this Latter House	$
54		CD-DVD	This Is That Time	$
55		CD-DVD	A Whole New Dimension of Dominion In Your Life	$
56		CD-DVD	Chosen For Glory	$
57		CD-DVD	Harvest Time for the Heirs of God	$
52		DVD	The Mystery of Man on the Sixth Day	$
DVD		DVD	Harvest Time for the Heirs of God	$

All VHS/DVD& Book are $20 each, CD's are $15 each, include $4 per item for shipping & handling. **Method of Payment** *(Be a good steward and operate with integrity and excellence. Your check will be electronically deposited so make sure funds are available in your account)* **You may also order online at www.wicctv.org.**

(Please Print Clearly)

Check/MO # _____   Check/MO Amt _____

Billing Name:_____

Credit Card _____ Mastercard _____ Visa _____ AMEX

Card # _____ Exp Date: _____

Total Amt: _____ Signature: _____

WorldWide International Campaign for Christ
P.O. Box 677276, Orlando FL 32867
866.924.WICC   wicctv.org

Product Order Form

Name: _____

Mailing Address: _____

City, ST & Zip: _____

Email Address: _____

Please indicate the type (VHS, CD, DVD)

Product #	Qty	Type	Description	Cost
12BK		Book	Reaching For The World	$
29			Mind & Mouth Determine Your Destiny	$
31			Give Me This Water	$
28			I Am Free	$
25			Power of the Promise	$
53		CD-DVD	The Glory of this Latter House	$
54		CD-DVD	This Is That Time	$
55		CD-DVD	A Whole New Dimension of Dominion In Your Life	$
56		CD-DVD	Chosen For Glory	$
57		CD-DVD	Harvest Time for the Heirs of God	$
52		DVD	The Mystery of Man on the Sixth Day	$
DVD		DVD	Harvest Time for the Heirs of God	$

All VHS/DVD& Book are $20 each, CD's are $15 each, include $4 per item for shipping & handling. **Method of Payment** *(Be a good steward and operate with integrity and excellence. Your check will be electronically deposited so make sure funds are available in your account)* **You may also order online at www.wicctv.org.**

(Please Print Clearly)

Check/MO # _____   Check/MO Amt _____

Billing Name: _____

Credit Card _____ Mastercard _____ Visa _____ AMEX

Card # _____ Exp Date: _____

Total Amt: _____ Signature: _____